"*Weekly Prayer Services for Parish Meetings,* edited by Marliss Ro̶̶̶̶ resource for working parish groups. It provides a scripturally b̶a̶s̶e̶d̶ structure that explicitly centers the meeting time in Christ. The contemporary prayers will deepen the bonds of faith. The use of the Sunday readings will provide a vital connection with the worship of the whole Church. The shared reflections and suggested questions encourage insights that will strengthen commitments to love and service with the community. I highly recommend this book for any continuing group in the parish."

Sydney Condray
Author, *Assembled In Christ*

"The two best things about the book are its adherence to the lectionary readings for the next Sunday and the way it builds in opportunities for shared reflection. With these two features, it enables users to begin a meditation that will culminate at the Sunday Eucharistic liturgy, and it provides opportunities for connecting the Sunday readings with daily life."

Dr. Mark F. Fischer, Ph.D.
Assistant Professor of Theology

"All of us who are called to leadership within the parish of the future are invited to become prayerful servant leaders. The prayer services in this book give us on-the-job training by calling us not to some token sign of prayer at the beginning of our meetings, but to an integrated experience in which we realize that we need to set aside a time of deeper prayer if we are to be disciples of Christ. The format is easy enough to follow and can enable even the most shy participant to experience ease in leading prayer.

"Included in the prayer services are the following attractive qualities: *The Call to Prayer* embraces creative use of the psalms, while *The Opening Prayer* sets the mood for the entire prayer experience. *The Readings* offers a balance between Old and New Testament choices. *The Shared Reflection* enables us to share our own faith stories and, at times, can serve as a practical parish corporate examination of conscience. It also leaves room to include specific parish issues. *Prayers at the End of the Meeting* shows a balance between basic rote prayers and more ingenious conversations from the heart. Throughout each prayer, there is the welcome use of inclusive language. All these qualities offer to our people a solid prayer outline as we call them to leadership positions in our parishes."

Dr. Celine Goessle, SCSC
Pastoral Administrator of St. Luke Parish
Bellaire, Michigan

WEEKLY
PRAYER
SERVICES

for
PARISH MEETINGS
Year C

MARLISS ROGERS, Editor

TWENTY-THIRD PUBLICATIONS
Mystic, Connecticut 06355

Acknowledgment: The quotations of the Bible used in this book are from the *New Revised Standard Version* (© 1989 Division of Christian Education of the National Council of Churches of Christ in the United States of America) and are reprinted with permission.

Second printing 1997

Twenty-Third Publications
185 Willow Street
P.O. Box 180
Mystic, CT 06355
(860) 536-2611
800-321-0411

ISBN 0-89622-599-2
Library of Congress Catalog Card Number 94-60153
Printed in the U.S.A.

Contents

WEEKLY
PRAYER
SERVICES
for
PARISH MEETINGS

Year C

Introduction

Prayer is an essential first item of business for every parish meeting. The parish council, the Saint Vincent de Paul Society, the festival planning committee, the liturgy board, the finance commission, and every other other parish organization or association has its own tasks and areas of expertise. But every parish group can function more effectively and with a greater sense of mission and purpose if its meeting begins and ends with a prayerful reminder that Christ is present where two or three have gathered in his name to continue his work.

Many excellent, hard-working parish council and committee members feel inadequate or inexperienced in leading prayer. The weekly lectionary-based prayer services in this book are intended to come to their rescue. Each complete prayer service has six elements:

Call to Prayer—assists people in focusing on the meeting and opening their hearts and minds to the presence and power of God

Opening Prayer—asks for the Lord's help and guides people's thoughts to the tasks at hand and the theme of that Sunday's scripture readings

Scripture Reading—presents one of the three readings from the Sunday lectionary for that week

Shared Reflection—encourages the participants to apply the reading to their own life, their parish, and the issues to be discussed at the meeting

Closing Prayer—summarizes the theme of the service and asks for the Lord's guidance during the meeting

Prayer at the End of the Meeting—recalls the theme of the prayer service and sends the meeting participants home and into the parish community with a sense of the Lord's presence and help.

Each service is arranged for three speakers (Leader, Reader 1, Reader 2) and the entire group (All), but this can be adapted to fit the needs of the group, the parish, the season, or the time allotted for the meeting. Permission is granted to reproduce the services in this book so that all meeting participants have their own copy.

It is recommended that the service be used during the week *prior* **to the Sunday on which the readings will be read at Mass.** When the prayer service focuses on the coming Sunday's readings, the meeting participants both pray for the guidance of the Spirit at their meeting, and prepare for next Sunday's proclamation of the Word.

The prayer services in this book were originally prepared for parish councils in the Archdiocese of Milwaukee as a service of the diocesan paper, the *Catholic Herald*. Many thanks go to Marliss Rogers, former co-director of the Office for Parish Councils in the Archdiocese of Milwaukee, who adapted the services for use in this book.

First Sunday of Advent

Call to Prayer (Light the candle for the first Sunday of Advent.)

Leader: We are gathered here as the people of God whose lives are centered in Christ. As we begin our Advent time, we affirm our faith in the Lord and invite Christ to be present at our meeting.

Opening Prayer

Leader: God of the sky and the earth, again we begin a season of waiting and wondering; a season of refinement. Continue the work you have begun in each of us and give us the strength and wisdom never to tire or grow weary. May we always find refreshment in you, through your Son and in the Holy Spirit, to whom we pray for ever and ever.

All: Amen.

Reading *Jeremiah 33:14–16*

Reader 1: The days are surely coming, says the LORD, when I will fulfill the promise I made to the house of Israel and the house of Judah. In those days and at that time I will cause a righteous Branch to spring up for David; and he shall execute justice and righteousness in the land. In those days Judah will be saved and Jerusalem will live in safety. And this is the name by which it will be called: "The LORD is our righteousness." **(Silent reflection)**

Shared Reflection

Reader 2: When we discuss the meaning of life and reflect on our experiences, we often fall back on everyday images to help us. One such common image is a tree. The expression, "a family tree," shows clearly how the offspring of one couple can branch out and flourish through many generations, like an acorn slowly becoming a great oak with innumerable branches. Similarly, the symbol of a tree can also help us understand a broad historical process. The image of a tree ties you and me today with the house of Israel and Judah, our ancestors in faith. We might call this a "religious tree," blossoming forth with the good news.

Leader: • What are the images that guide your life?
• What personal image from your life relates to this season of Advent?
• Is there a guiding image that assists your parish during this season of refinement?

Closing Prayer

Leader: God of light, even amid darkness, keep our roots strong and true to your love. Never let us rot in despair or bitterness. Let us always seek the comfort of your word and action exhibited by someone who also belongs to this "religious tree." Let us take a moment to identify any needs among us and give them over to God.

(Spontaneous petitions)

We ask these prayers through Christ our Lord.

All: Amen.

Prayer at the End of the Meeting

Leader: Let us join hands and pray the Lord's Prayer together.

All: Our Father...

Reprinted with permission from *Weekly Prayer Services for Parish Meetings, Cycle C.* © 1994 *Catholic Herald*, Archdiocese of Milwaukee. Twenty-Third Publications, P.O. Box 180, Mystic, CT 06355. 800-321-0411

Second Sunday of Advent

Call to Prayer (Light two candles on the Advent wreath.)

Leader: We have come together to give ourselves to the Lord and to serve God's people. It is through who we are and what we do that others will come to know God. As we begin our prayer time, we pause to reflect for a moment on this call to serve the people of God.

Opening Prayer

Leader: God of light and wisdom, this season of darkness reminds each of us of our need for you, the light of the world. During this Advent time, give us a special grace to be sensitive to those areas in our lives that need refinement. We make our lives acceptable only in you, through your Son Jesus, and in the Holy Spirit, to whom we pray, for ever and ever.

All: Amen.

Reading *Luke 3:1–6*

Reader 1: In the fifteenth year of the reign of Emperor Tiberius, when Pontius Pilate was governor of Judea, and Herod was ruler of Galilee, and his brother Philip ruler of the region of Ituraea and Trachonitis, and Lysanias ruler of Abilene, during the high priesthood of Annas and Caiaphas, the word of God came to John son of Zechariah in the wilderness. He went into all the region around the Jordan, proclaiming a baptism of repentance for the forgiveness of sins, as it is written in the book of the words of the prophet Isaiah, "The voice of one crying out in the wilderness: 'Prepare the way of the Lord, make his paths straight. Every valley shall be filled, and every mountain and hill shall be made low, and the crooked shall be made straight, and rough ways made smooth; and all flesh shall see the salvation of God.'" **(Silent reflection)**

Shared Reflection

Reader 2: Advent reminds us of the need to keep telling the story of our faith again and again. When it comes to data and factual information, the story told by Luke is detailed. He could win the religion category on "Jeopardy" easily. But more than a cold list of facts, Luke's story tells us of continuity, trust, and hope in a world that is often short of these virtues. We, too, are the instruments of hope as we make ready a path for the savior.

Leader: • What stories can be told about this parish that speak of trust and hope?
  • How are we refining our parish story to meet the needs of our own time?

Closing Prayer

Leader: God of kindness and goodness, protect us as we face changes in our lives. May the stories of our faith guide all our decisions and influence us today. Let us take a moment to remember anyone who has died and whose memory continues to influence us.

(Everyone is invited to mention deceased parishioners, friends, or family members by name.)

We give these people to you, God.

All: Amen.

Prayer at the End of the Meeting

Leader: Let us close our time together by praying the Lord's Prayer.

All: Our Father...

Reprinted with permission from *Weekly Prayer Services for Parish Meetings, Cycle C.* © 1994 *Catholic Herald,* Archdiocese of Milwaukee. Twenty-Third Publications, P.O. Box 180, Mystic, CT 06355. 800-321-0411

Third Sunday of Advent

Call to Prayer (Light three candles on the Advent wreath.)

Leader: As we gather this evening for our meeting, let us set aside distractions and open ourselves to the enlightenment we need to discern how we can best serve both God and one another as we begin tonight's meeting.

Opening Prayer

Leader: Lord God, through your Son Jesus you teach us to value the ultimate victory over death. As we prepare to celebrate the birth of a gentle baby, we are also reminded of the sufferings that Jesus had to undergo. That is why Jesus is our source of strength. We pray confidently in his name, Jesus Christ, for ever and ever.

All: Amen.

Reading *Zephaniah 3:14–18*

Reader 1:   Sing aloud, O daughter Zion; shout, O Israel! Rejoice and exult with all your heart, O daughter Jerusalem! The Lord has taken away the judgments against you, he has turned away your enemies. The King of Israel, the Lord, is in your midst; you shall fear disaster no more. On that day it shall be said to Jerusalem: Do not fear, O Zion; do not let your hands grow weak. The Lord, your God, is in your midst, a warrior who gives victory; he will rejoice over you with gladness, he will renew you in his love; he will exult over you with loud singing as on a day of festival. I will remove disaster from you, so that you will not bear reproach for it. **(Silent reflection)**

Shared Reflection

Reader 2:   The championship game in any sport creates, in a special way, a heightened sense of excitement both for the players and the spectators. The contrast is striking, however, after the game when one glimpses the jubilant winner's locker room and then switches over to the somber losers in their locker room. While Zephaniah is reminding us in general of our experience with both success and failure, he is particularly emphasizing our final victory. To continue the sports analogy, even with all the struggles in life, we know we are on the "championship team" when we are one with God.

Leader: •Does this group discuss both the positives and negatives of the parish? Do we emphasize one more than the other?
•What does it take to look honestly at all sides of a problem or issue?

Closing Prayer

Leader: Loving God, bless our time together. Let our actions ensure that our winning is not done in arguments and debates but in our union with you. Let us mention some of the pressing needs in our parish and world.

(Spontaneous petitions)

We ask these things through Christ our Lord.

All: Amen.

Prayer at the End of the Meeting

Leader: Together, let us join hands and pray the Lord's Prayer.

All: Our Father...

Reprinted with permission from *Weekly Prayer Services for Parish Meetings, Cycle C.* © 1994 *Catholic Herald,* Archdiocese of Milwaukee. Twenty-Third Publications, P.O. Box 180, Mystic, CT 06355. 800-321-0411

Fourth Sunday of Advent

Call to Prayer (Light all four candles on the Advent wreath.)

Leader: As we approach the joyous feast of Christmas and the end of our time of waiting and stillness, we pray for an increased awareness of the needs of others and for the grace to be caring, compassionate people in the spirit of the gospel.

Opening Prayer

Leader: Loving and gentle God, in our waiting and anticipation we trust that we are never alone. The presence of your Son within us reminds us that we do not walk our life's journey alone. Fill this room with the bond of community that the loneliness we sometimes feel may never last long. We pray this through Jesus Christ, in the Spirit, one God, for ever and ever.

All: Amen.

Reading *Luke 1:39–45*

Reader 1: In those days Mary set out and went with haste to a Judean town in the hill country, where she entered the house of Zechariah and greeted Elizabeth. When Elizabeth heard Mary's greeting, the child leaped in her womb. And Elizabeth was filled with the Holy Spirit and exclaimed with a loud cry, "Blessed are you among women, and blessed is the fruit of your womb. And why has this happened to me, that the mother of my Lord comes to me? For as soon as I heard the sound of your greeting, the child in my womb leaped for joy. And blessed is she who believed that there would be a fulfillment of what was spoken to her by the Lord." **(Silent reflection)**

Shared Reflection

Reader 2: Each of us knows, in a way perhaps unique to ourselves, what it is to feel alone. Luke tells us this week that Mary "went with haste" to visit her cousin Elizabeth. This seems to suggest how alone Mary may have felt with the burden of the Annunciation, and how much she needed to confide in someone. We can imagine her asking herself who will believe what the angel had told her and what she had consented to do. We can sense God's presence when Mary finally arrived and talked to Elizabeth. That sense of Mary's loneliness makes us echo the Magnificat. God did wonderful things for her and for Elizabeth. So, too, in our need God also cares for us.

Leader: • How do you handle loneliness?
• How does this parish bring people together in ways more significant than just being in the same room?

Closing Prayer

Leader: Lord God, soften the loneliness within each of us. We know it is part of life yet we need to be reminded of the perspective that we are always waiting for the fullness of your love. Let us take a moment to identify any intentions that are present.

(Spontaneous petitions)

We ask these prayers through Christ our Lord.

All: Amen.

Prayer at the End of the Meeting

Leader: The fourth week of Advent focuses on Mary. Let us close by reciting together the prayer that was inspired by her Annunciation, the Hail Mary.

All: Hail Mary…

Reprinted with permission from *Weekly Prayer Services for Parish Meetings, Cycle C.* © 1994 *Catholic Herald*, Archdiocese of Milwaukee. Twenty-Third Publications, P.O. Box 180, Mystic, CT 06355. 800-321-0411

Epiphany

Call to Prayer

Leader: Praise God with shouts of joy, all people.

All: Praise God with shouts of joy, all people.

Leader: Sing to the glory of his name.

All: Sing to the glory of his name.

Leader: Say to God, "How wonderful are the things you do. Your power is so great that your enemies bow down before you."

All: Your power is so great that your enemies bow down before you.

Leader: Lord, everyone on earth worships you.

All: They sing praises to you. They sing praises to your name.
(Based on Psalm 66)

Opening Prayer

Leader: Creator God, you alone give light to our darkness. You are the light, and you shine with splendor all the days of human history. Give light to our eyes and hearts so that we see and respond to your inspiration. We ask this through Christ our Lord.

All: Amen.

Reading *Matthew 2:1–12*

Reader 1: In the time of King Herod, after Jesus was born in Bethlehem of Judea, wise men from the East came to Jerusalem, asking, "Where is the child who has been born king of the Jews? For we observed his star at its rising, and have come to pay him homage." When King Herod heard this, he was frightened, and all Jerusalem with him; and calling together all the chief priests and scribes of the people, he inquired of them where the Messiah was to be born. They told him, "In Bethlehem of Judea; for so it has been written by the prophet: 'And you, Bethlehem, in the land of Judah, are by no means least among the rulers of Judah; for from you shall come a ruler who is to shepherd my people Israel.'" Then Herod secretly called for the wise men and learned from them the exact time when the star had appeared. Then he sent them to Bethlehem, saying, "Go and search diligently for the child; and when you have found him, bring me word so that I may also go and pay him homage." When they had heard the king, they set out; and there, ahead of them, went the star that they had seen at its rising, until it stopped over the place where the child was. When they saw that the star had stopped, they were overwhelmed with joy. On entering the house, they saw the child with Mary his mother, and they knelt down and paid him homage. Then, opening their treasure chests, they offered him gifts of gold, frankincense, and myrrh. And having been warned in a dream not to return to Herod, they left for their own country by another road. **(Silent reflection)**

Shared Reflection

Reader 2: Matthew's story is packed with adventure—the Magi seek and find and are transformed; Herod exemplifies the brutality of power; the Holy Family takes refuge in a strange land. By the light of a mysterious star, Jesus is given to the whole world.

Leader: •How do we present Jesus to the world by the way we live our lives?
•What does our parish do to assist refugees and victims of political oppression?

Closing Prayer

All: Dear Lord, you were visited by angels and by kings, but no one pleased you more than your own mother and father. Help us to follow the stars you send into our lives. When we find you, Jesus, like the kings, we will prostrate ourselves in adoration and thanksgiving. Amen.

Prayer at the End of the Meeting

All: It has been our privilege, dear Lord, to work for the coming of your kingdom. Thank you for the invitation to be here where you were in our midst. We praise you, adore you, and love you with all our hearts. Bless our work for your kingdom. We ask this in your name, Jesus. Amen.

Reprinted with permission from *Weekly Prayer Services for Parish Meetings, Cycle C.* © 1994 *Catholic Herald*, Archdiocese of Milwaukee. Twenty-Third Publications, P.O. Box 180, Mystic, CT 06355. 800-321-0411

Baptism of the Lord

Call to Prayer

Leader: Let the house of Israel say, "His mercy endures forever."
Let the house of Aaron say, "His mercy endures forever."
Let those who fear the Lord say, "His mercy endures forever."

All: Give thanks to the Lord. His love is everlasting.

Leader: The stone which the builders rejected has become the cornerstone.
By the Lord has this been done; it is wonderful in our eyes.

All: Give thanks to the Lord. His love is everlasting.
(Based on Psalm 118)

Opening Prayer

Leader: God, our loving Father, you bless us and trust us with your creation.

All: Give us the grace to return your love, and to be faithful to you for a lifetime. We ask this through Christ our Lord. Amen.

Reading *Luke 3:15–16, 21–22*

Reader 1: As the people were filled with expectation, and all were questioning in their hearts concerning John, whether he might be the Messiah, John answered all of them by saying, "I baptize you with water; but one who is more powerful than I is coming; I am not worthy to untie the thong of his sandals. He will baptize you with the Holy Spirit and fire." Now when all the people were baptized, and when Jesus also had been baptized and was praying, the heaven was opened, and the Holy Spirit descended upon him in bodily form like a dove. And a voice came from heaven, "You are my Son, the Beloved; with you I am well pleased." **(Silent reflection)**

Shared Reflection

Reader 2: All of us must act responsibly in caring for ourselves and in caring for our aged parents and others. We do not have an absolute right over our lives. God is the author of life, and God decides when that life should flow out into eternal life with him. We commit ourselves to respect and cherish life in all persons at all ages.

Leader: •Can you identify service to helpless persons as an act of service to God? As fastening his sandal? God said of Jesus, "You are my beloved Son." Could God say that, in some sense, of each of us? Is he beloved of us?

Closing Prayer

Leader: Lord, we want to be fit to loosen your sandal and the sandals of those with whom we live and with whom we work.

All: Teach us to live in the presence of your Spirit. Descend on us, Holy Spirit. We believe in you and desire to be faithful to the Father, to Jesus, and to you.

Prayer at the End of the Meeting

Leader: Thank you, dear Lord, for inviting us to work for your kingdom. It is a privilege to be in your service. Bless our work and our families. We ask this in the name of Jesus.

All: Amen.

Reprinted with permission from *Weekly Prayer Services for Parish Meetings, Cycle C.* © 1994 *Catholic Herald*, Archdiocese of Milwaukee. Twenty-Third Publications, P.O. Box 180, Mystic, CT 06355. 800-321-0411

Second Sunday in Ordinary Time

Call to Prayer

Leader: All-powerful God, you honored your Son through the miracle at Cana. You also introduced us to Mary's influence with you and your Son.

All: We praise you, loving God, for this epiphany of your Son's power and for the honor bestowed on Mary.

Leader: Mary, Mother of God, you called your Son's attention to the distress of your hosts and asked him to intercede.

All: We honor and praise you, Mother of God. Give us the courage to trust in Jesus, your Son.

Opening Prayer

Leader: Nations shall behold your vindication, and all kings your glory. You shall be a glorious crown in the hand of the Lord. We ourselves behold your glory, and we praise you, O God. Teach us to be attentive and faithful. We ask this through your Son, Jesus Christ our Lord.

All: Amen.

Reading *John 2:1–12*

Reader 1:   On the third day there was a wedding in Cana of Galilee, and the mother of Jesus was there. Jesus and his disciples had also been invited to the wedding. When the wine gave out, the mother of Jesus said to him, "They have no wine." And Jesus said to her, "Woman, what concern is that to you and to me? My hour has not yet come." His mother said to the servants, "Do whatever he tells you." Now standing there were six stone water jars for the Jewish rites of purification, each holding twenty or thirty gallons. Jesus said to them, "Fill the jars with water." And they filled them up to the brim. He said to them, "Now draw some out, and take it to the chief steward." So they took it. When the steward tasted the water that had become wine, and did not know where it came from (though the servants who had drawn the water knew), the steward called the bridegroom and said to him, "Everyone serves the good wine first, and then the inferior wine after the guests have become drunk. But you have kept the good wine until now." Jesus did this, the first of his signs, in Cana of Galilee, and revealed his glory; and his disciples believed in him. After this he went down to Capernaum with his mother, his brothers, and his disciples; and they remained there a few days. **(Silent reflection)**

Shared Reflection

Reader 2: Many parishes are served by the members of organizations like the Saint Vincent de Paul Society. These generous people figuratively turn water into wine by giving hope to the poorest members of their parish and their neighborhood.

Leader: • Are you presently giving of your time, talent, or treasure to someone less fortunate than yourself?
• Recall a story of a family celebration during which sharing or healing took place.

Closing Prayer

Leader: Dear Lord, we often envy the rich and the powerful, and spend great amounts of energy accumulating wealth. But God looks past our bank account to our acts of service, sharing, and charity. Fortunes from the stock exchange will wither like the grass in a summer drought. God, help us to choose that which lasts forever. We ask this through Christ our Lord.

All: Amen.

Prayer at the End of the Meeting

Leader: Dear Lord, thank you for the invitation to work for your kingdom. It is a privilege to be in your service. We praise you, adore you, and love you with all our hearts. Bless our work and our families. Be with us today and always.

All: Amen.

Reprinted with permission from *Weekly Prayer Services for Parish Meetings, Cycle C.* © 1994 *Catholic Herald*, Archdiocese of Milwaukee. Twenty-Third Publications, P.O. Box 180, Mystic, CT 06355. 800-321-0411

Third Sunday in Ordinary Time

Call to Prayer

Leader: Today is holy to the Lord your God. Do not be sad. Do not weep. Rejoicing in the Lord must be your strength.

All: Amen.

Opening Prayer

Leader: Heavenly Father, we often feel like failures. But when we are in sorrow and doubt, you come to us, you comfort us, and you call us to renew our trust in you.

All: We renew our trust in you, Lord, and we thank you for your ever-lasting concern for us.

Reading *Luke 1:1–4; 4:14–21*

Reader 1: Since many have undertaken to set down an orderly account of the events that have been fulfilled among us, just as they were handed on to us by those who from the beginning were eyewitnesses and servants of the word, I too decided, after investigating everything carefully from the very first, to write an orderly account for you, most excellent Theophilus, so that you may know the truth concerning the things about which you have been instructed. Then Jesus, filled with the pow-er of the Spirit, returned to Galilee, and a report about him spread through all the surrounding country. He began to teach in their syn-agogues and was praised by everyone. When he came to Nazareth, where he had been brought up, he went to the synagogue on the sab-bath day, as was his custom. He stood up to read, and the scroll of the prophet Isaiah was given to him. He unrolled the scroll and found the place where it was written: "The Spirit of the Lord is upon me, because he has anointed me to bring good news to the poor. He has sent me to proclaim release to the captives and recovery of sight to the blind, to let the oppressed go free, to proclaim the year of the Lord's favor." And he rolled up the scroll, gave it back to the attendant, and sat down. The eyes of all in the synagogue were fixed on him. Then he began to say to them, "Today this scripture has been fulfilled in your hearing." **(Silent reflection)**

Shared Reflection

Reader 2: Jesus returned to his hometown to announce his mission. Just as Jesus was filled with the Holy Spirit, so we, too, beg that the Spirit of the Lord be upon us so we can be faithful to our Christian mission. We are called to contribute to the good of society, just as Christ went about doing good, healing the sick, and restoring sight to the blind.

Leader: • Are you bringing glad tidings (the good news) to the poor?
• How central is Jesus' mission to our parish community?

Closing Prayer

Leader: Jesus, we genuinely desire to be good news for others; we want to release those held captive by sin and ignorance; we long to give sight to those around us who are blind to injustice and pain. Holy Spirit, live in us; direct our days; make us people of virtue.

All: Amen.

Prayer at the End of the Meeting

Leader: Dear Lord, it is a privilege to be invited to work for your kingdom. Thank you for calling us to this mission. We praise, adore, and love you with all our hearts. Bless our work and our families. We ask this through Christ our Lord.

All: Amen.

Reprinted with permission from *Weekly Prayer Services for Parish Meetings, Cycle C.* © 1994 *Catholic Herald,* Archdiocese of Milwaukee. Twenty-Third Publications, P.O. Box 180, Mystic, CT 06355. 800-321-0411

Fourth Sunday in Ordinary Time

Call to Prayer

Leader: We are your people, Lord, and we praise you.

All: Teach us the meaning of justice and mercy.

Leader: May the Spirit of the Lord be upon us.

All: Now and forever. Amen.

Opening Prayer

All: God of time, past and present, we gather again in your name and for your purposes. Be with us in our prayer and discussion. May they be pleasing to you, and may we always seek to know you in humility and faithfulness. Amen.

Reading *1 Corinthians 12:31–13:13*

Reader 1:   But strive for the greater gifts. And I will show you a still more excellent way. If I speak in the tongues of mortals and of angels, but do not have love, I am a noisy gong or a clanging cymbal. And if I have prophetic powers, and understand all mysteries and all knowledge, and if I have all faith, so as to remove mountains, but do not have love, I am nothing. If I give away all my possessions, and if I hand over my body so that I may boast, but do not have love, I gain nothing. Love is patient; love is kind; love is not envious or boastful or arrogant or rude. It does not insist on its own way; it is not irritable or resentful; it does not rejoice in wrongdoing, but rejoices in the truth. It bears all things, believes all things, hopes all things, endures all things. Love never ends. But as for prophecies, they will come to an end; as for tongues, they will cease; as for knowledge, it will come to an end. For we know only in part, and we prophesy only in part; but when the complete comes, the partial will come to an end. When I was a child, I spoke like a child, I thought like a child, I reasoned like a child; when I became an adult, I put an end to childish ways. For now we see in a mirror, dimly, but then we will see face to face. Now I know only in part; then I will know fully, even as I have been fully known. And now faith, hope, and love abide, these three; and the greatest of these is love. **(Silent reflection)**

Shared Reflection

Reader 2:   To look silly in front of others can be a very embarrassing moment. Remember the "Gong Show"? If the judges didn't like someone's zany act, the "clanging cymbal" was clearly heard. In this Sunday's second reading, Saint Paul says that we should act our age or else we will sound like a clanging cymbal. Childhood is the time to decide who possesses the best toys and who has the strongest dad. In adulthood, we put those comparisons behind us and celebrate our oneness and maturity in Christ.

Leader: • In conversations, can you discern gossip from gospel?
• What do your adult relationships mean to you?
• How can our parish put an end to any "childish ways" that are present here and now?

Closing Prayer

All: God of past and present, you are with us in the midst of all times and situations, both happy and sad. Help us to grab hold of what matters: living our lives in love and justice. Free us from silly judgments and quick assumptions about others that only keep us childish. Open us to the beauty that can be found in each person. We pray this through Christ our Lord. Amen.

Prayer at the End of the Meeting

Leader: Creator God, as we leave this meeting and return to home and family, may we take you with us. Guide us during this week, that we will have the energy and courage to implement all that we have decided upon today. Help us never to be just clanging cymbals, making noise rather than the joyful praise of your goodness. May we always seek a childlike faith that trusts in your love for us.

All: Amen.

Reprinted with permission from *Weekly Prayer Services for Parish Meetings, Cycle C*. © 1994 *Catholic Herald*, Archdiocese of Milwaukee. Twenty-Third Publications, P.O. Box 180, Mystic, CT 06355. 800-321-0411

Fifth Sunday in Ordinary Time

Call to Prayer

Leader: Let the House of Israel say, "His mercy endures forever."
Let the House of Aaron say, "His mercy endures forever."
Let those who fear the Lord say, "His mercy endures forever."

All: Give thanks to the Lord. His love is everlasting.
(Based on Psalm 118)

Opening Prayer

Leader: Loving God, you bless us and trust us with your creation. Give us the grace to return your love, and to be faithful to you for our entire life-time. We ask this through Christ our Lord.

All: Amen.

Reading *Luke 5:1–11*

Reader 1: Once while Jesus was standing beside the lake of Gennesaret, and the crowd was pressing in on him to hear the word of God, he saw two boats there at the shore of the lake; the fishermen had gone out of them and were washing their nets. He got into one of the boats, the one belonging to Simon, and asked him to put out a little way from the shore. Then he sat down and taught the crowds from the boat. When he had finished speaking, he said to Simon, "Put out into the deep water and let down your nets for a catch." Simon answered, "Master, we have worked all night long but have caught nothing. Yet if you say so, I will let down the nets." When they had done this, they caught so many fish that their nets were beginning to break. So they signaled their partners in the other boat to come and help them. And they came and filled both boats, so that they began to sink. But when Simon Peter saw it, he fell down at Jesus' knees, saying, "Go away from me, Lord, for I am a sinful man!" For he and all who were with him were amazed at the catch of fish that they had taken; and so also were James and John, sons of Zebedee, who were partners with Simon. Then Jesus said to Simon, "Do not be afraid; from now on you will be catching people." When they had brought their boats to shore, they left everything and followed him. **(Silent reflection)**

Shared Reflection

Reader 2: When Jesus called the first apostles to become "fishers of people" he didn't have to worry about employment rules or personnel policies.

But today the church must give every evidence of being a just employer, in witness to gospel principles and as a credible example for all employers.

Leader: •If you are an employer, are you committed to justice in your dealings with employees?
•Have you experienced injustice from church employers?
•What recommendations can you make to those employers?

Closing Prayer

All: We pray, dear Lord, for all here present, and all who serve you tonight in the work of your kingdom. We thank you for the full catch of fish, and for the invitation to follow you. Like Simon and his companions, we will remain alert to hear your call, to live your values in our lives, and to carry them into the marketplace. We adore you, Lord, and love you with all our hearts. Amen.

Prayer at the End of the Meeting

Leader: Dear Lord, it was a privilege to be here with all these good people. We will stay the course, and try to be ever more generous in response to your invitation. Bless our work here and bless our families.

All: Amen.

Reprinted with permission from *Weekly Prayer Services for Parish Meetings, Cycle C.* © 1994 *Catholic Herald*, Archdiocese of Milwaukee. Twenty-Third Publications, P.O. Box 180, Mystic, CT 06355. 800-321-0411

Sixth Sunday in Ordinary Time

Call to Prayer

Leader: Blessed is the one who trusts in the Lord.

All: Whose hope is in the Lord.

Leader: That one is like a tree planted beside the waters.

All: That stretches out its roots to the stream.

Leader: It fears not the heat when it comes.

All: Its leaves stay green.

Leader: In the year of drought it shows no distress.

All: But still bears fruit.
(Based on Psalm 1)

Opening Prayer

Leader: O God, we trust in your promises. We believe that you will be faithful to your covenant. We want to live by the Beatitudes, even when we are rejected and ridiculed for doing so. We are proud to be in your company, to be your disciples. We need you and beg for your grace.

All: We ask this through Christ your Son. Amen.

Reading *Luke 6:17; 20–26*

Reader 1: He came down with them and stood on a level place, with a great crowd of his disciples and a great multitude of people from all Judea, Jerusalem, and the coast of Tyre and Sidon. Then he looked up at his disciples and said: "Blessed are you who are poor, for yours is the kingdom of God. Blessed are you who are hungry now, for you will be filled. Blessed are you who weep now, for you will laugh. Blessed are you when people hate you, and when they exclude you, revile you, and defame you on account of the Son of Man. Rejoice in that day and leap for joy, for surely your reward is great in heaven; for that is what their ancestors did to the prophets. But woe to you who are rich, for you have received your consolation. Woe to you who are full now, for you will be hungry. Woe to you who are laughing now, for you will mourn and weep. Woe to you when all speak well of you, for that is what their ancestors did to the false prophets." **(Silent reflection)**

Shared Reflection

Reader 2: It is not easy to live the Beatitudes. It is especially difficult to suffer persecution or rejection because of what we believe. Throughout the history of the church, people have been persecuted and even lost their lives for taking a stand for justice, for the poor, and for the oppressed. In the gospel, these are called the "blessed ones."

Leader: •Can you think of a time when you were ridiculed or otherwise insulted because you were a Catholic with strong faith or values?
•Have you ever ridiculed anyone of another faith when your beliefs differed from those of the other person?

Closing Prayer

Leader: Dear Lord, make us strong and faithful. Do not let rejection, insult, or ridicule shake our fidelity to you. It is an honor to be among your disciples. Regardless of what others call us, we want always to be called "blessed" by you.

All: Amen.

Prayer at the End of the Meeting

Leader: It is a privilege and a joy to serve in your company, Lord, even when others belittle us and persecute us for trying to live your gospel. Make us strong and faithful. We want to be among the "blessed" for all eternity. Stay at our side, Lord.

All: We ask this through Christ who is God's Son. Amen.

Reprinted with permission from *Weekly Prayer Services for Parish Meetings, Cycle C.* © 1994 *Catholic Herald*, Archdiocese of Milwaukee. Twenty-Third Publications, P.O. Box 180, Mystic, CT 06355. 800-321-0411

Seventh Sunday in Ordinary Time

Call to Prayer

Leader: Praise God with shouts of joy, all people!

All: Praise God with shouts of joy, all people!

Leader: Sing to the glory of his name.

All: Sing to the glory of his name.

Leader: Say to God, "How wonderful are the things you do."

All: Your power is so great that your enemies bow down before you.

Leader: Everyone on earth worships you. They sing praises to you.

All: They sing praises to your name.
(Based on Psalm 66)

Opening Prayer

Leader: God, our Creator, we know that you are never outdone in generosity. You call us sons and daughters, and ask us to be compassionate and generous in mercy and forgiveness. We desire to have, but know that only with your gracious help can we give or receive in good measure, pressed down, shaken together, running over. We ask for your spirit of generosity and we beg this in the name of Christ your Son.

All: Amen.

Reading *Luke 6:27–38*

Reader 1: "But I say to you that listen, Love your enemies, do good to those who hate you, bless those who curse you, pray for those who abuse you. If any one strikes you on the cheek, offer the other also; and from anyone who takes away your coat do not withhold even your shirt. Give to everyone who begs from you; and if anyone takes away your goods, do not ask for them again. Do to others as you would have them do to you. If you love those who love you, what credit is that to you? For even sinners love those who love them. If you do good to those who do good to you, what credit is that to you? For even sinners do the same. If you lend to those from whom you hope to receive, what credit is that to you? Even sinners lend to sinners, to receive as much again. But love your enemies, do good, and lend, expecting nothing in return. Your reward will be great, and you will be children of the Most High; for he is kind to the ungrateful and the wicked. Be merciful, just as your Father is merciful. Do not judge, and you will not be judged; do not condemn, and you will not be condemned. Forgive, and you will be forgiven; give, and it will be given to you. A good measure, pressed down, shaken together, running over, will be put into your lap; for the measure you give will be the measure you get back." **(Silent reflection)**

Shared Reflection

Reader 2:   This passage from Luke's gospel presents several of Jesus' most challenging instructions to his disciples. What could be more difficult than loving those who hate us? "Do unto others..." is such an important value it has been called the Golden Rule. At times the Golden Rule seems somewhat tarnished.

Leader: •How do we practice the Golden Rule in our families?
•How does our parish reach out in love and concern to those who are in need of hearing the good news?

Closing Prayer

Leader: God, our Father, your Son Jesus taught us to expect forgiveness from you in the degree that we grant mercy and forgiveness to others. We want to be forgiving people, and we want to be able to pray the Lord's Prayer with integrity. We need your help to accomplish this, and we ask for it through Christ your Son.

All: Amen.

Prayer at the End of the Meeting

Leader: Aware of our failures and our need for forgiveness, we pray.

All: Our Father...

Reprinted with permission from *Weekly Prayer Services for Parish Meetings, Cycle C.* © 1994 *Catholic Herald,* Archdiocese of Milwaukee. Twenty-Third Publications, P.O. Box 180, Mystic, CT 06355. 800-321-0411

Eighth Sunday in Ordinary Time

Call to Prayer

Leader: We approach the Lenten season with the joy that is the mark of a Christian. Just as the dormant season of winter holds the hope of new life in the spring, our desert journey through Lent contains the seeds of our new life with the resurrected Lord. **(Moment of silence)**

Opening Prayer

Leader: Let us pray.

All: Loving God, we are a pilgrim people in a secular world that often demeans everything we value as we journey to the Promised Land. Risen Lord, we are an Easter people encouraged by your example; we sacrifice to do your will. Holy Spirit, we are a priestly people who humbly ask your guidance as we help build your kingdom here on earth. Amen.

Reading *1 Corinthians 15:54–58*

Reader 1: When this perishable body puts on imperishability, and this mortal body puts on immortality, then the saying that is written will be fulfilled: "Death has been swallowed up in victory." "Where, O death, is your victory? Where, O death, is your sting?" The sting of death is sin, and the power of sin is the law. But thanks be to God, who gives us the victory through our Lord Jesus Christ. Therefore, my beloved, be steadfast, immovable, always excelling in the work of the Lord, because you know that in the Lord your labor is not in vain. **(Silent reflection)**

Shared Reflection

Reader 2: The readings this week remind us that our speech, our behavior, and our intentions should bear witness to our solidarity with the poor and the love of our enemies, which are the conditions of discipleship. Paul uses balance, logic, and poetic imagery to demonstrate the intensity of his message. He ends with a sobering call for action. "Steadfast," "persevering," "immovable," and "not in vain" speak Paul's conviction that the Lord's work is a matter of life and death.

Leader: • What prevents us from persevering in the Lord's work?
• What preparation does our parish provide for those who take discipleship seriously?

Closing Prayer

All: Triune God, we are open to your will. Guide our deliberations tonight. May the work we do in your honor draw us closer to each other and to you, in the name of your Son, our savior, Jesus the Christ. Amen.

Prayer at the End of the Meeting *(Serenity Prayer)*

All: God, grant me serenity to accept the things I cannot change, courage to change the things I can, and wisdom to know the difference; living one day at a time, enjoying one moment at a time; accepting hardship as a pathway to peace; taking, as Jesus did, this sinful world as it is, not as I would have it; trusting that you will make all things right if I surrender to your will; so that I may be reasonably happy in this life and supremely happy with you in the next. Amen.

Reprinted with permission from *Weekly Prayer Services for Parish Meetings, Cycle C.* © 1994 *Catholic Herald,* Archdiocese of Milwaukee. Twenty-Third Publications, P.O. Box 180, Mystic, CT 06355. 800-321-0411

Ninth Sunday in Ordinary Time

Call to Prayer

Leader: O God, come to our assistance.

All: Lord, make haste to help us. Glory be to the Father, and to the Son, and to the Holy Spirit, as it was in the beginning, is now, and ever shall be, world without end. Amen.

Opening Prayer

Leader: Let us pray.

All: Eternal God, we gather in your name to continue learning about your wonderful deeds. Keep us open to your message of forgiveness and mercy for ourselves and especially for others. We ask this through Christ our Lord. Amen.

Reading *Galatians 1:1–2, 6–10*

Reader 1:   Paul an apostle—sent neither by human commission nor from human authorities, but through Jesus Christ and God the Father, who raised him from the dead—and all the members of God's family who are with me, To the churches of Galatia: I am astonished that you are so quickly deserting the one who called you in the grace of Christ and are turning to a different gospel—not that there is another gospel, but there are some who are confusing you and want to pervert the gospel of Christ. But even if we or an angel from heaven should proclaim to you a gospel contrary to what we proclaimed to you, let that one be accursed! As we have said before, so now I repeat, if anyone proclaims to you a gospel contrary to what you received, let that one be accursed! Am I now seeking human approval, or God's approval? Or am I trying to please people? If I were still pleasing people, I would not be a servant of Christ. **(Silent reflection)**

Shared Reflection

Reader 2:   This passage marks the beginning of Paul's dynamic letter to the Galatians. Paul doesn't live in the world of today where there are over sixty cable channels and more magazines and newspapers than there are fish to wrap. His message is strong, yet simple, and very applicable to our own times: Cherish what you believe and beware of those who try to dissuade you. Worry only about pleasing God!

Leader: •How can we be tolerant of others while still holding to our particular beliefs?

- How does our parish utilize communication media in service of the gospel?
- Are we ever guilty of altering the gospel by our actions?

Closing Prayer

All: We are created in your image, gracious God. Open our minds and hearts to the variety of opinions and insights shared around this table today. May we not feel we have to protect each statement we make, but trust that your presence will guide our dialogue. Help us to be particularly thoughtful of one another as we go about our work. Amen.

Prayer at the End of the Meeting

Leader: As we prepare to return to our everyday lives, we pause to give God thanks.

All: Trusting in the promises you made to us, Loving God, may we leave this place a little more confident and a little more compassionate toward others. Help us to remember that it is your approval we seek as we continue our faith journey. Lead us to your kingdom of love and peace. Amen.

Reprinted with permission from *Weekly Prayer Services for Parish Meetings, Cycle C.* © 1994 *Catholic Herald*, Archdiocese of Milwaukee. Twenty-Third Publications, P.O. Box 180, Mystic, CT 06355. 800-321-0411

First Sunday of Lent

Call to Prayer

All: Loving God, how much you must love us to redeem us through your Son! You give Jesus to us as an example of how to live. May our self-denial and self-sacrifice during this Lenten season bring us closer to you at Easter than we are right now. Let this Lent be a time for us to focus on our spirituality, and on our role in the redemptive process as we work together to do your will. **(Moment of silence)**

Opening Prayer

Leader: Let us pray. Lord, come into our hearts.

All: And make them your own.

Leader: Lord, we praise you for your glory.

All: May our work tonight bear witness to that praise.

Leader: Lord, we thank you for gifting us to serve you.

All: May we use our gifts to further your kingdom.

Leader: Lord, we ask for guidance.

All: May our deliberations and decisions be wise and just.

Reading *Luke 4:1–13*

Reader 1: Jesus, full of the Holy Spirit, returned from the Jordan and was led by the Spirit in the wilderness, where for forty days he was tempted by the devil. He ate nothing at all during those days, and when they were over, he was famished. The devil said to him, "If you are the Son of God, command this stone to become a loaf of bread." Jesus answered him, "It is written, 'One does not live by bread alone.'" Then the devil led him up and showed him in an instant all the kingdoms of the world. And the devil said to him, "To you I will give their glory and all this authority; for it has been given over to me, and I give it to anyone I please. If you, then, will worship me, it will all be yours." Jesus answered him, "It is written, 'Worship the Lord your God, and serve only him.'" Then the devil took him to Jerusalem, and placed him on the pinnacle of the temple, saying to him, "If you are the Son of God, throw yourself down from here, for it is written, 'He will command his angels concerning you, to protect you,' and 'On their hands they will bear you up, so that you will not dash your foot against a stone.'" Jesus answered him, "It is said, 'Do not put the Lord your God to the test.'" When the devil had finished every test, he departed from him until an opportune time. **(Silent reflection)**

Shared Reflection

Reader 2: How appropriate this reading is for Lent! Christ's victory over temptation foreshadows his victory over death. Jesus' preparation for his messianic mission is a model for our observance of Lent: Self-denial and self-sacrifice are a means of resisting temptation and increasing our sanctity.

Leader: • What can we glean from the words of Luke to help us make this Lent a means of greater personal holiness?
• What can our parish do at this late date to make Lent more meaningful for everyone?

Closing Prayer

All: Heavenly God, you love us so much that you sacrificed your only Son. Lord Jesus, you chose death to atone for our sins. Holy Spirit, you strengthen us to resist temptation and strive for holiness. Triune God, we gratefully acknowledge your presence among us tonight. Free us from temptations of personal glory in order to work together in a spirit of consensus to further your kingdom. In light of eternity, it doesn't matter whose idea it is, Lord, as long as your will is done. In Jesus' name we pray. Amen.

Prayer at the End of the Meeting (*Prayer of Saint Francis*)

All: Lord, make me an instrument of your peace.
Where there is hatred, let me sow love;
where there is injury, pardon;
where there is doubt, faith;
where there is despair, hope;
where there is darkness, light;
and where there is sadness, joy.

Divine Master,
grant that I may not so much seek
to be consoled as to console;
to be understood as to understand;
to be loved as to love.
For it is in giving that we receive;
it is in pardoning that we are pardoned;
and it is in dying that we are born to eternal life.
Amen.

Reprinted with permission from *Weekly Prayer Services for Parish Meetings, Cycle C.* © 1994 *Catholic Herald,* Archdiocese of Milwaukee. Twenty-Third Publications, P.O. Box 180, Mystic, CT 06355. 800-321-0411

Second Sunday of Lent

Call to Prayer

All: Heavenly Father, you have called us to service, to be fruitful laborers sowing the seeds of love and light in the world. We are thankful for the blessings of responsibility. **(Moment of silence)**

Opening Prayer

Leader: Lord, we praise you for your glory.

All: May our work tonight bear witness to that praise.

Reading *Luke 9:28–36*

Reader 1:   Now about eight days after these sayings Jesus took with him Peter and John and James, and went up on the mountain to pray. And while he was praying, the appearance of his face changed, and his clothes became dazzling white. Suddenly they saw two men, Moses and Elijah, talking to him. They appeared in glory and were speaking of his departure, which he was about to accomplish at Jerusalem. Now Peter and his companions were weighed down with sleep; but since they had stayed awake, they saw his glory and the two men who stood with him. Just as they were leaving him, Peter said to Jesus, "Master, it is good for us to be here; let us make three dwellings, one for you, one for Moses, and one for Elijah"—not knowing what he said. While he was saying this, a cloud came and overshadowed them; and they were terrified as they entered the cloud. Then from the cloud came a voice that said, "This is my Son, my Chosen; listen to him!" When the voice had spoken, Jesus was found alone. And they kept silent and in those days told no one any of the things they had seen. **(Silent reflection)**

Shared Reflection

Reader 2:   Like the apostles, we can fall into a deep sleep and miss the significance of our experience of Christ in the world. Then when we awaken, we witness but don't participate in the mystery. We sense in this reading the feeling of exclusion in Peter's frantic last-minute effort to set up tents in order to keep Moses and Elijah from departing. Peter wanted to cling to the feeling of awe that the sleeping trio felt upon awakening to the glorified vision. As they were caught up in the cloud that overshadowed them they grew fearful, but they were calmed by the warm and loving words of God expressing pride in Jesus.

Leader: •How do we assist all parishioners, women as well as men, children as well as adults, old as well as young, to participate fully in the activities of our parish?

• How do we, like Peter, apply human (and sometimes humorous) solutions to profound issues like that of women's role in the church?

Closing Prayer

All: Triune God, we gratefully acknowledge your presence among us tonight. Free us from temptations of personal glory or self-aggrandizement to work together in a spirit of consensus to further your kingdom. In light of eternity, it doesn't matter whose idea it is, Lord, as long as your will is done. In Jesus' name we pray. Amen.

Prayer at the End of the Meeting

Leader: This week's reading reminds us of the glory of God, and so we pray:

All: Glory be to the Father, and to the Son, and to the Holy Spirit, as it was in the beginning, is now, and ever shall be, world without end. Amen.

Reprinted with permission from *Weekly Prayer Services for Parish Meetings, Cycle C.* © 1994 *Catholic Herald,* Archdiocese of Milwaukee. Twenty-Third Publications, P.O. Box 180, Mystic, CT 06355. 800-321-0411

Third Sunday of Lent

Call to Prayer

All: Heavenly Father, we seek to be a caring and understanding people. Breathe into the decisions we will make during our meeting the Spirit of your nearness. Through your grace, help us to carry out our ministry of leadership in reconciling and understanding ways. **(Moment of silence)**

Opening Prayer

Leader: Let us pray. Lord, come into our hearts.

All: And make them your own.

Leader: Lord, we ask for guidance.

All: May our deliberations and decisions be wise and just.

Reading *1 Corinthians 10:1–6, 10–12*

Reader 1: I do not want you to be unaware, brothers and sisters, that our ancestors were all under the cloud, and all passed through the sea, and all were baptized into Moses in the cloud and in the sea, and all ate the same spiritual food, and all drank the same spiritual drink. For they drank from the spiritual rock that followed them, and the rock was Christ. Nevertheless, God was not pleased with most of them, and they were struck down in the wilderness. Now these things occurred as examples for us, so that we might not desire evil as they did. And do not complain as some of them did, and were destroyed by the destroyer. These things happened to them to serve as an example, and they were written down to instruct us, on whom the ends of the ages have come. So if you think you are standing, watch out that you do. **(Silent reflection)**

Shared Reflection

Reader 2: This reading is a call to repentance and a warning of the consequences of the failure to repent. Although Paul speaks like a parent wagging his finger at an errant child, his compassion shows through. He exhorts the people of Corinth to learn from the mistakes of their ancestors: "If you think you are standing, watch out that you do not fall." The Israelites, Paul says, "all ate the same spiritual food. All drank the same spiritual drink." But they had wicked desires and grumbled so they were struck down. This is not how people in Christian communities should behave. A Washington, D.C., pastor suggests that the sacraments guide our parish life: "The sacraments are the Catholic Church's ticket into people's hearts....People don't want to just join; they want to belong...."

Leader: • How ready is our parish to see conversion as an ongoing responsibility and to be the sacramental presence of Jesus Christ in a world of broken bodies?

• Are we open to all people—the handicapped? immigrants? persons with AIDS? drug addicts?

• Is our parish having a good time being a parish? Is there laughter?

Closing Prayer

All: Heavenly God, you love us so much that you sacrificed your only Son. Lord Jesus, you accepted death to atone for our sins. Holy Spirit, you guide us on the path to greater holiness. Help us to work together in a spirit of consensus to further your kingdom and see that your will is done. Amen.

Prayer at the End of the Meeting *(Prayer of Saint Francis)*

All: Lord, make me an instrument of your peace.
Where there is hatred, let me sow love;
where there is injury, pardon;
where there is doubt, faith;
where there is despair, hope;
where there is darkness, light;
and where there is sadness, joy.

Divine Master,
grant that I may not so much seek
to be consoled as to console,
to be understood as to understand;
to be loved as to love.
For it is in giving that we receive;
it is in pardoning that we are pardoned;
and it is in dying that we are born to eternal life.
Amen.

Reprinted with permission from *Weekly Prayer Services for Parish Meetings, Cycle C.* © 1994 *Catholic Herald*, Archdiocese of Milwaukee. Twenty-Third Publications, P.O. Box 180, Mystic, CT 06355. 800-321-0411

Fourth Sunday of Lent

Call to Prayer

All: We recognize our human weaknesses and the effects of original sin. But we claim our baptismal birthright as God's sons and daughters, whose inheritance was won for us by the blood of Jesus, our brother. With joy, we proclaim our trust in God's fidelity and assistance in all our earthly tasks. **(Moment of silence)**

Opening Prayer

Leader: Let us pray.

All: God in heaven, we are an Easter people. Buoyed by the hope of redemption we endure our desert journey through Lent. Jesus, our brother, we thank you for humbling yourself to take our nature and teach us how to live. Gentle Spirit, we ask for wisdom as we make decisions tonight for your glory and the furthering of the kingdom, in the name of Jesus Christ. Amen.

Reading *2 Corinthians 5:17–21*

Reader 1: So if anyone is in Christ, there is a new creation: everything old has passed away; see, everything has become new! All this is from God, who reconciled us to himself through Christ, and has given us the ministry of reconciliation; that is, in Christ, God was reconciling the world to himself, not counting their trespasses against them, and entrusting the message of reconciliation to us. So we are ambassadors for Christ, since God is making his appeal through us; we entreat you on behalf of Christ, be reconciled to God. For our sake he made him to be sin who knew no sin, so that in him we might become the righteousness of God. **(Silent reflection)**

Shared Reflection

Reader 2: Joy characterizes the readings this week, from the celebration of the first Passover in the Promised Land to the father's initiative in forgiving the prodigal son. Paul celebrates the same initiative as he announces our new creation in Christ. He calls us to rejoice because God has reconciled us to himself through Christ and has given us the ministry of reconciliation. We are called to forgive others as God forgives us—unconditionally. Forgiveness is an act of the will; it often takes our emotions a while to catch up with our spirit of forgiveness. Reconciliation implies a mending of the relationship that requires a change of heart by the offender. If there is no change of heart, there is no reconciliation but there can still be forgiveness.

Leader: • Recall your experiences of forgiving and being forgiven. How did forgiveness make a difference?

• If I, as the offender, ask for forgiveness and it is denied, is there forgiveness? Is there reconciliation?

Closing Prayer

All: Ever faithful God, we dare to call you "Father." We implore your counsel in our deliberations tonight. Open us to see each other's viewpoints. Inspire us to stretch our imaginations to find creative solutions to increasing problems on shrinking budgets. Guide us and all your children to move, as the Israelites did, from dependence to mature independence and to see our work for the church as a means of personal spiritual growth. This we ask in the name of your Son, our savior, Jesus Christ. Amen.

Prayer at the End of the Meeting

Leader: Let us join hands in solidarity and pray for the spirit of forgiveness as we say the Lord's Prayer.

All: Our Father...

Reprinted with permission from *Weekly Prayer Services for Parish Meetings, Cycle C.* © 1994 *Catholic Herald,* Archdiocese of Milwaukee. Twenty-Third Publications, P.O. Box 180, Mystic, CT 06355. 800-321-0411

Fifth Sunday of Lent

Call to Prayer

All: As we near Easter and the coming spring, we are surrounded by lingering signs of winter's death, yet we already anticipate with joy spring's new life! May all our deliberations and dialogue lead to renewed life for our parish community. **(Moment of silence)**

Opening Prayer

Leader: Let us pray.

All: Lord God, fill us with a spirit of honesty and openness. Let us be honest and true admitting that you are our strength. We praise you for opening our eyes and hearts to the needs of people around us, and for challenging us to accept them and help them without making judgments about them. Bless our deliberations today and always. Amen.

Reading *John 8:1–11*

Reader 1: Then each of them went home, while Jesus went to the Mount of Olives. Early in the morning he came again to the temple. All the people came to him and he sat down and began to teach them. The scribes and the Pharisees brought a woman who had been caught in adultery; and making her stand before all of them, they said to him, "Teacher, this woman was caught in the very act of committing adultery. Now in the law Moses commanded us to stone such women. Now what do you say?" They said this to test him, so that they might have some charge to bring against him. Jesus bent down and wrote with his finger on the ground. When they kept on questioning him, he straightened up and said to them, "Let anyone among you who is without sin be the first to throw a stone at her." And once again he bent down and wrote on the ground. When they heard it, they went away, one by one, beginning with the elders; and Jesus was left alone with the woman standing before him. Jesus straightened up and said to her, "Woman, where are they? Has no one condemned you?" She said, "No one, sir." And Jesus said, "Neither do I condemn you. Go your way, and from now on do not sin again." **(Silent reflection)**

Shared Reflection

Reader 2: It is clear from Jesus' words that he believed the woman had the power within her to change her sinful ways. His final words of forgiveness and healing cut off the woman from her past, propelling her into a future where God is doing something new. We, too, have the power within us to change and open our hearts so that God can do something new with us. This reading challenges us to look at our intolerance. A half century after World War II, there are unhealed wounds from the Holocaust. Survivors and victims' families still grieve that more religious leaders didn't protest the deportation of Jews to concentration camps. African Americans still experience discrimination more than a century after the Civil War. We are challenged to begin a new wave of education to combat racism, to forgive and forget, to see all people as brothers and sisters.

Leader: •Recall an experience of forgiving and being forgiven. How did forgiveness make a difference?
•What can we as a parish do to combat discrimination?

Closing Prayer

All: Ever faithful God, we implore your counsel in our deliberations tonight. Open us to see each other's viewpoints. Guide us to be more tolerant of people who are different from us. Inspire us to love the sinner while hating the sin as your Son Jesus did. We make our prayer in his name. Amen.

Prayer at the End of the Meeting *(Prayer of Saint Francis)*

All: Lord, make me an instrument of your peace.
Where there is hatred, let me sow love;
where there is injury, pardon;
where there is doubt, faith;
where there is despair, hope;
where there is darkness, light;
and where there is sadness, joy.

Divine Master,
grant that I may not so much seek
to be consoled as to console,
to be understood as to understand;
to be loved as to love.
For it is in giving that we receive;
it is in pardoning that we are pardoned;
and it is in dying that we are born to eternal life.
Amen.

Reprinted with permission from *Weekly Prayer Services for Parish Meetings, Cycle C.* © 1994 *Catholic Herald,* Archdiocese of Milwaukee. Twenty-Third Publications, P.O. Box 180, Mystic, CT 06355. 800-321-0411

Palm Sunday

Call to Prayer

All: May our hearts be open to the exultation of the Lord; may our love be multiplied from the heart and even to the lips, to bring forth fruit to the Lord, a holy life, and to talk with watchfulness in his light. (Eighth Song, Odes of Solomon)

Opening Prayer

Leader: Let us pray.

All: Strengthen us, Lord God, during this week when we remember Jesus' final journey to Jerusalem. Guide our thoughts, words, and actions that we might bring about the New Jerusalem, your kingdom of peace and harmony, in our parish, our neighborhood, and our world. Amen.

Reading *Luke 19:28–40*

Reader 1: After he had said this, he went on ahead, going up to Jerusalem. When he had come near Bethphage and Bethany, at the place called the Mount of Olives, he sent two of the disciples, saying, "Go into the village ahead of you, and as you enter it you will find tied there a colt that has never been ridden. Untie it and bring it here. If anyone asks you, 'Why are you untying it?' just say this, 'The Lord needs it.'" So those who were sent departed and found it as he had told them. As they were untying the colt, its owners asked them, "Why are you untying the colt?" They said, "The Lord needs it." Then they brought it to Jesus; and after throwing their cloaks on the colt, they set Jesus on it. As he rode along, people kept spreading their cloaks on the road. As he was now approaching the path down from the Mount of Olives, the whole multitude of the disciples began to praise God joyfully with a loud voice for all the deeds of power that they had seen, saying, "Blessed is the king who comes in the name of the Lord! Peace in heaven, and glory in the highest heaven!" Some of the Pharisees in the crowd said to him, "Teacher, order your disciples to stop." He answered, "I tell you, if these were silent, the stones would shout out." **(Silent reflection)**

Shared Reflection

Reader 2: This passage describes Jesus' journey to Jerusalem to face the painful yet triumphant destiny that awaits him there. What an amazing story! The plan unfolded just as Jesus told the disciples it would; they felt secure being with their Master in spite of all the things he had told them about his impending suffering and death. How thrilled the disciples must have been with the reception Jesus received! The people used their cloaks to create a carpet for him like they would for royalty. Luke translates their shouts of "hosanna" as "Peace in heaven and glory in the highest," an obvious allusion to the angel's nativity song. The Pharisees fear Roman vengeance to this pretender-king for "there is no king but Caesar." But, like an uncapped champagne bottle, this flow of spontaneous jubilation simply cannot be stopped.

Leader: • Recall an experience of exploding spontaneity in your own life which contained elements of awe.
• How was this experience like an encounter with God?

Closing Prayer

All: Ever faithful God, inspire us to stretch our imaginations to find creative solutions to increasing problems. Guide us and all your children to move, as the Israelites did, from dependence to mature independence and to see our work for the church as a means of personal spiritual growth. This we ask in the name of your Son, our Savior, Jesus Christ. Amen.

Prayer for the End of the Meeting

Leader: Christ became obedient for us.

All: Even unto death on the cross.

Leader: We adore you, O Christ, and we praise you.

All: Because by your holy cross, you have redeemed the world.

Reprinted with permission from *Weekly Prayer Services for Parish Meetings, Cycle C.* © 1994 *Catholic Herald*, Archdiocese of Milwaukee. Twenty-Third Publications, P.O. Box 180, Mystic, CT 06355. 800-321-0411

Easter Sunday

Call to Prayer

All: During this week of sacred and solemn celebration, our hearts are filled with thankfulness and joy. May we truly learn the lesson of love which Jesus has taught us by his life and death, and carry it into our lives and ministry.

Opening Prayer

Leader: Let us pray.

All: Jesus is risen. Alleluia!
He has appeared to the women at the tomb. Alleluia!
We have experienced him in the breaking of the bread. Alleluia!
Like Thomas we proclaim, "My Lord and my God." Alleluia!

Reading *Colossians 3:1–4*

Reader 1: So if you have been raised with Christ, seek the things that are above, where Christ is, seated at the right hand of God. Set your minds on things that are above, not on things that are on earth, for you have died, and your life is hidden with Christ in God. When Christ who is your life is revealed, then you also will be revealed with him in glory. **(Silent reflection)**

Shared Reflection

Reader 2: On Easter Sunday we begin fifty days of rejoicing during which time we reflect on the post-resurrection manifestations of Jesus, the consequences for us of his death and resurrection, and the life of the church where he continues to be present. In this reading, Paul reminds us that Jesus has not risen alone; we, too, are empowered to rise with him! That is this day's good news. More than celebrating an historical event, Easter announces the mysterious reality that we already have been raised up. There is joy in this reality, but it also places a moral imperative on us. We must live as people touched by the resurrection. While Jesus' resurrection can seem long ago and far away, mini-resurrections can touch us every day. We have all experienced the dyings and risings of everyday life. A case of the doldrums can be magically cured by a visit from a joyful friend, who becomes for us at that moment "Jesus with skin."

Leader: •Have you ever experienced "Jesus with skin"?
•What can we do in our parish and community to demonstrate that we live like people who are risen with Christ?

Closing Prayer

All: Risen Savior, King of Glory, you come among us today in mystery. You share with us your death and rising. While we await your final coming in glory, open our hearts and minds to see your resurrected presence in people, in nature, in the church community, and in the events of our daily lives. Let our deliberations tonight awaken us to your resurrection. We ask this in the name of the Father and of the Son and of the Holy Spirit. Amen.

Prayer for the End of the Meeting

Leader: Christians, to the Pascal Victim
Offer your thankful praises...

All: Christ indeed from death is risen,
our new life obtaining.
Have mercy, victor King, ever reigning!
Amen. Alleluia.
(Adapted from the Sequence of Easter Sunday)

Reprinted with permission from *Weekly Prayer Services for Parish Meetings, Cycle C.* © 1994 *Catholic Herald,* Archdiocese of Milwaukee. Twenty-Third Publications, P.O. Box 180, Mystic, CT 06355. 800-321-0411

Second Sunday of Easter

Call to Prayer

(Place a green or flowering plant in the center of the meeting table to symbolize growth.)

Leader: The Easter season is a fifty-day period of rejoicing. During this time we reflect on the post-resurrection manifestations of Jesus, the consequences for us of his death and resurrection, and the life of the church where he remains present. We call ourselves into the presence of God, releasing the cares of the day and clearing our minds for the tasks before us tonight. **(Moment of silence)**

Opening Prayer

Leader: Let us pray.

All: Sweet Jesus, you took our nature and came humbly into our world as a helpless baby; may we balance our innocence with wisdom as we confront the problems of a secular society without being tainted by it. Crucified Christ, you took our sin and reconciled us in your blood; may we accept life's hardships as pathways to peace secure in the belief that our salvation is through the cross. Risen Lord, you proved you are God by overcoming death; may we prove we are Christians by our joyful attitude in the face of adversity because our hearts are set on higher realms. We pray confidently in your name. Amen.

Reading *Acts of the Apostles 5:12–16*

Reader 1: Now many signs and wonders were done among the people through the apostles. And they were all together in Solomon's Portico. None of the rest dared to join them, but the people held them in high esteem. Yet more than ever believers were added to the Lord, great numbers of both men and women, so that they even carried out the sick into the streets, and laid them on cots and mats, in order that Peter's shadow might fall on some of them as he came by. A great number of people would also gather from the towns around Jerusalem, bringing the sick and those tormented by unclean spirits, and they were all cured. **(Silent reflection)**

Shared Reflection

Reader 2: In the previous chapter of Acts, the community joined Peter and John in praying that signs and wonders would accompany the proclamation of the gospel. Here Luke recounts an answer to that prayer. The apostles are presented as the cornerstones of the community because of the power they have manifested. Without a doubt, many were drawn to the community because of the healings that took place through Peter and the apostles. Of course, they were simply the conduit for the divine power which flowed to those in need of physical or spiritual healing. "Shadow" in the New Testament always demonstrates divine power. Any healing the apostles did simply mirrored the healings of Jesus who often used physical healing as a means to spiritual healing. He shocked the Pharisees by forgiving the sins of those he cured. Sometimes, in our own lives, an experience of physical or psychological illness calls us to reevaluate our spiritual condition and pray for wholeness again.

Leader: •Recall a time of physical illness in your own life when your vulnerability and powerlessness called you to examine your relationship with God.

•Are there opportunities within our congregation to use illness as a means of spiritual healing?

Closing Prayer

Leader: Creator God, we sing your praise with joy for the miracle of creation! Healing Lord, we thank you for the miracle of forgiveness you extend to us and model for us. All-knowing Spirit, we implore your wisdom as we discern truth and direction in building your kingdom. In the name of the Trinity we pray. Amen.

Prayer at the End of the Meeting

All: Dear God, we believe that where two or more are gathered in your name, you are in our midst. We believe that we have encountered you in our gathering tonight. May this encounter reach deeply into our hearts as we leave this place and touch the lives of others. May we be signs of the presence of the risen Lord, today and always. Amen.

Reprinted with permission from *Weekly Prayer Services for Parish Meetings, Cycle C.* © 1994 *Catholic Herald*, Archdiocese of Milwaukee. Twenty-Third Publications, P.O. Box 180, Mystic, CT 06355. 800-321-0411

Third Sunday of Easter

Call to Prayer

Leader: Prayer is the wellspring of wisdom that guides us as we conduct the business of the meeting. In prayerful silence, let us reflect on the Easter mystery and make a personal act of faith in the risen Lord's power to affect our deliberations. **(Silent reflection)**

Opening Prayer

All: Loving God, you will that all people be saved and come to the knowledge of your truth. Through the Easter mysteries just celebrated, may we have the courage to proclaim your gospel to all people and may we advance in the way of salvation and love. We make this prayer through Christ our Lord.

Reading *Acts of the Apostles 5:27–32, 40–41*

Reader 1: When they had brought them, they had them stand before the council. The high priest questioned them, saying, "We gave you strict orders not to teach in this name, yet here you have filled Jerusalem with your teaching and you are determined to bring this man's blood on us." But Peter and the apostles answered, "We must obey God rather than any human authority. The God of our ancestors raised up Jesus, whom you had killed by hanging him on a tree. God exalted him at his right hand as Leader and Savior that he might give repentance to Israel and forgiveness of sins. And we are witnesses to these things, and so is the Holy Spirit whom God has given to those who obey him." And when they had called in the apostles, they had them flogged. Then they ordered them not to speak in the name of Jesus, and let them go. As they left the council, they rejoiced that they were considered worthy to suffer dishonor for the sake of the name. **(Silent reflection)**

Shared Reflection

Reader 2: Peter is not being anti-semitic. The statement, "Jesus whom you had killed," is made to dramatize for his listeners the radical nature of Jesus' death and resurrection. He also issues a command to obey and be loyal to Christ. On a scale of 1 to 10, where does our loyalty register? We have to ask ourselves about our commitment, our determination to be faithful to family, friends, associates — to say nothing of fidelity to Christ. Much in our daily media challenges our loyalties. We are called by Christ continually to reexamine, to purify, to strengthen those loyalties asked of us by Christ. "It is God rather than human beings whom we must obey." There often is a price for loyalty: The officers beat the apostles and warned them not to speak in the name of Jesus. They left "rejoicing that they were considered worthy to suffer dishonor for the sake of the name."

Leader: •Can we name our successes and failures in being loyal to God rather than to human beings?
•How do we sift, judge, discern, and choose the gospel call?
•How can hope derived from this Easter season of grace be a support to us?

Closing Prayer

Leader: Let us bring a close to our prayer.

All: God in heaven, we thank you for those times when we remained faithful against tempting odds, and we ask forgiveness for the times when we were weak and cowardly. Keep us close to you. We recommit ourselves to fidelity to the only One who can be our ultimate and never-failing strength. One act of fidelity to you and to our associates gives strength for a second and third act of loyalty. We ask for the grace we need to be faithful now and always through Christ our Lord. Amen.

Prayer at the End of the Meeting

All: Dear God, we believe that we have encountered you in this gathering. May this encounter enable us to touch the lives of others. May we be signs of the presence of the risen Lord to others, we pray in the name of Jesus. Amen.

Reprinted with permission from *Weekly Prayer Services for Parish Meetings, Cycle C.* © 1994 *Catholic Herald*, Archdiocese of Milwaukee. Twenty-Third Publications, P.O. Box 180, Mystic, CT 06355. 800-321-0411

Fourth Sunday of Easter

Call to Prayer

Leader: As we gather for our meeting, we seek the Lord's wisdom and guidance. We need to put aside the cares and concerns of the day and open our hearts to God in prayer, so that we may discover God's will in our deliberations.

Opening Prayer

All: Most glorious God, you sent Jesus into the world to be our true light. Awaken in us and in all people the truth of faith. May all people be born again to new life in baptism and enter the fellowship of your kingdom. Grant our prayer through your risen Son, Jesus Christ. Amen.

Reading *John 10:27–30*

Reader 1: My sheep hear my voice. I know them and they follow me. I give them eternal life, and they will never perish. No one will snatch them out of my hand. What my father has given me is greater than all else, and no one can snatch it out of the Father's hand. The Father and I are one. **(Silent reflection)**

Shared Reflection

Reader 2: The relationship between the shepherd and his sheep is a truly mutual one. The shepherd's livelihood depends on the well-being of the sheep, and he is constantly watchful to protect and care for them. Like Jesus, the Good Shepherd, we are called to bring God's love and compassion to others. Our protection must extend to refugees and those who are persecuted in their own countries.

Leader: •How does our parish care for people in the community, including those who are not members of the parish?
•What can we do to be more caring, compassionate leaders?
•How can we make our country's leaders more aware of the need for compassion in dealing with refugees?

Closing Prayer

All: God, our Creator, Redeemer, and Sanctifier, you have brought us closer to you through the death and resurrection of Jesus and have strengthened and comforted us through your spirit of love. May we honor you through the love which we bear for one another and which is tested in action. We ask this through Christ, our Lord, now and for ever. Amen.

Prayer at the End of the Meeting

All: Holy Lord, you have blessed our meeting with your presence. We leave now to take up our responsibility for the tasks which make up our daily work. May you always be praised in our efforts to build our parish into a faithful, hopeful, and loving community. Amen.

Reprinted with permission from *Weekly Prayer Services for Parish Meetings, Cycle C.* © 1994 *Catholic Herald*, Archdiocese of Milwaukee. Twenty-Third Publications, P.O. Box 180, Mystic, CT 06355. 800-321-0411

Fifth Sunday of Easter

Call to Prayer

Leader: Let us begin with a period of silence during which we each can put aside the cares and concerns of the day and open our hearts to the Lord in prayer, so that we may discover God's will in our deliberations. **(Moment of silence)**

Opening Prayer

All: Lord and Source of all gifts, we rejoice in the fullness of your holy generosity. We thank you especially now for the gift of newness that comes each year in the springtime. May our hearts continue to grow in your love as we continue our journey to a new kingdom. Lord, you are forever fresh and new, yet forever the same. Blessed are you, Lord our God, who bestows new life on us. Amen.

Reading *John 13:31–35*

Reader 1:   When [Judas] had gone out, Jesus said, "Now the Son of Man has been glorified, and God has been glorified in him. If God has been glorified in him, God will also glorify him in himself and will glorify him at once. Little children, I am with you only a little longer. You will look for me; and as I said to the Jews so now I say to you, 'Where I am going, you cannot come.' I give you a new commandment, that you love one another. Just as I have loved you, you also should love one another. By this everyone will know that you are my disciples, if you have love for one another." **(Silent reflection)**

Shared Reflection

Reader 2:   Jesus tells us that it is love for each other that distinguishes us as his disciples, an agape love that will transform us and transform the community as well. Service to the community must be rooted in a strong prayer life, for it is God's plan that we are carrying out, not our own.

Leader: •How can loving others transform us?
•How can love transform our community?
•What is the relationship between service and prayer?

Closing Prayer

All: Loving God, in every age you raise up models of love, compassion, and service. In this age we look to people like Mother Teresa of Calcutta; centuries before they praised Vincent de Paul for his love of the poor.

Strengthen us to embody their example in our works of charity. We ask this through Christ our Lord, who was raised from the dead after giving his life on the Cross in service of all people. Amen.

Prayer at the End of the Meeting

All: O God of loveliness, O Lord of heaven above, journey forth from this place with us and strengthen us so that we may proclaim your love to others in thoughts, words, and actions. We make this prayer inspired by the Spirit who is love. Amen.

Reprinted with permission from *Weekly Prayer Services for Parish Meetings, Cycle C.* © 1994 *Catholic Herald,* Archdiocese of Milwaukee. Twenty-Third Publications, P.O. Box 180, Mystic, CT 06355. 800-321-0411

Sixth Sunday of Easter

Call to Prayer

Leader: Let us begin by praying the Sign of the Cross and calling to mind how these simple and oft-repeated words and actions are a reminder of the salvation won by Jesus Christ which we celebrate throughout this Easter season.

All: In the name of the Father, and of the Son, and of the Holy Spirit. Amen.

Opening Prayer

All: Blessed are you, Lord God, for through your goodness you have given us this holy season. May our lives give you honor, our mouths proclaim your goodness, our hands be instruments of your compassion, and our hearts offer you a home, now and for ever. Amen.

Reading *John 14:23–29*

Reader 1: Jesus said, "Those who love me will keep my word, and my Father will love them, and we will come to them and make our home with them. Whoever does not love me does not keep my words; and the word that you hear is not mine, but is from the Father that sent me. I have said these things to you while I am still with you. But the Advocate, the Holy Spirit, whom the Father will send in my name, will teach you everything, and remind you of all that I have said to you. Peace I leave with you; my peace I give to you. I do not give to you as the world gives. Do not let your hearts be troubled, and do not let them be afraid. You heard me say to you, 'I am going away, and I am coming to you.' If you loved me, you would rejoice that I am going to the Father, because the Father is greater than I. And now I have told you this before it occurs, so that when it does occur, you may believe." **(Silent reflection)**

Shared Reflection

Reader 2: Jesus promises the disciples a profound kind of peace that will take anxiety and fear from their hearts and sustain them through the difficult times to come, as they carry on Jesus' ministry in the world. As Christians, we also experience the peace of Christ as the gift of his abiding spirit. Now it is up to us to extend this peace to all who are needy or broken. The world is hungry for the peace of Christ!

Leader: •What is the difference between the world's peace and the peace that is given by Jesus?
•How are we extending the peace of Jesus to our neighborhoods and community?

Closing Prayer

All: God, our Creator, Redeemer, and Sanctifier, may we honor you through the love and peace which we bear for one another and which is tested in action. We ask this through Christ, our Lord, now and for ever. Amen.

Prayer at the End of the Meeting *(Prayer of Saint Francis)*

All: Lord, make me an instrument of your peace.
Where there is hatred, let me sow love;
where there is injury, pardon;
where there is doubt, faith;
where there is despair, hope;
where there is darkness, light;
and where there is sadness, joy.

Divine Master,
grant that I may not so much seek
to be consoled as to console,
to be understood as to understand;
to be loved as to love.
For it is in giving that we receive;
it is in pardoning that we are pardoned;
and it is in dying that we are born to eternal life.
Amen.

Reprinted with permission from *Weekly Prayer Services for Parish Meetings, Cycle C.* © 1994 *Catholic Herald*, Archdiocese of Milwaukee. Twenty-Third Publications, P.O. Box 180, Mystic, CT 06355. 800-321-0411

Seventh Sunday of Easter

Call to Prayer

Leader: Let us be open to God's presence in our midst.

All: May our hearts receive God's Word.

Leader: The Lord gives us strength.

All: The Lord blesses us with peace.

Opening Prayer

All: Risen Lord, as we gather for our meeting, we seek your wisdom and guidance. We stray when we seek our own solutions and rewards at the expense of our community, our family, or our world. Renew us in the truth of your love so we can celebrate your mercy and continue to live our lives according to your plan. Amen.

Reading *John 17:20–26*

Reader 1: "I ask not only on behalf of these, but also on behalf of those who will believe in me through their word, that they may all be one. As you, Father, are in me as I am in you, may they also be in us, so that the world may believe that you have sent me. The glory that you have given me I have given them, so that they may be one, as we are one, I in them and you in me, that they may become completely one, so that the world may know that you have sent me and have loved them even as you have loved me. Father, I desire that those also, whom you have given me, may be with me where I am, to see my glory, which you have given me because you loved me before the foundation of the world. Righteous Father, the world does not know you, but I know you; and these know that you have sent me. I made your name known to them, and I will make it known, so that the love with which you have loved me may be in them, and I in them." **(Silent reflection)**

Shared Reflection

Reader 2: Jesus prayed that God's love might be in the hearts of his followers to unite them and prepare them for their mission. Our mission in the church today is the same as that of the disciples: to minister to one another and create a community of Christian living. Sometimes the "stuff" we consider so important is really a distraction in our service to God. This week, let us renew ourselves in the simple truth of God's love and guidance.

Leader: •How do we bring God's love to the people of our community?
•How can we cultivate the unity for which Jesus prayed?

Closing Prayer

All: God of all peoples and all nations, Lord of all creatures great and small, make us one in your spirit. Let our deliberations be peaceful and a source of unity. Let our actions reflect your unconditional love for all. We ask this through Jesus Christ, the savior of all nations. Amen.

Prayer at the End of the Meeting

Leader: Holy Lord, may the Spirit you bestowed on your church to begin the teaching of the gospel continue to work in the world through the hearts of all who believe.

All: We ask this through Christ our Lord who lives and reigns with the Creator and the Holy Spirit, one God, forever and ever. Amen.

Reprinted with permission from *Weekly Prayer Services for Parish Meetings, Cycle C.* © 1994 *Catholic Herald,* Archdiocese of Milwaukee. Twenty-Third Publications, P.O. Box 180, Mystic, CT 06355. 800-321-0411

Pentecost

Call to Prayer

Leader: Our meeting time is truly kingdom-building time. We call ourselves into the presence of God, clear our minds of the cares of the day, prepare ourselves for the tasks before us, and contemplate the sacred mystery of how the same Spirit entered the Upper Room long ago and dwells in our midst today. **(Moment of silence)**

Opening Prayer

Leader: Let us pray.

All: Loving God, you gave us your Son for our salvation and your Spirit for our guidance; may we be open to your ways. Sacrificial Lamb, you left us the eucharist for our supernatural nourishment; may we use it often to remain united with you. Holy Spirit, you gift each of us according to the Divine Plan; may we be willing to use our gifts in God's service. We pray confidently in the name of the triune God. Amen.

Reading *1 Corinthians 12:3–7, 12–13*

Reader 1:   Therefore I want you to understand that no one speaking by the Spirit of God ever says "Let Jesus be cursed!" and no one can say "Jesus is Lord" except by the Holy Spirit. Now there are varieties of gifts, but the same Spirit; and there are varieties of services, but the same Lord; and there are varieties of activities, but it is the same God who activates all of them in everyone. To each is given the manifestation of the Spirit for the common good. For just as the body is one and has many members, and all the members of the body, though many, are one body, so it is with Christ. For in the one Spirit we were all baptized into one body—Jews or Greeks, slaves or free—and we were all made to drink of one Spirit. **(Silent reflection)**

Shared Reflection

Reader 2:   Paul's message is uncompromising and authoritative. The Corinthian community is divided around the very reality that should be the source of their unity: the Spirit. Only God's Spirit, Paul insists, not the false spirits of the pagan community, enables us to profess Jesus as Lord. Perhaps we, too, need to be reminded that we need the gifts of the Spirit to fulfill the variety of ministries in our parish communities. We have the willingness to serve, or we wouldn't be here. But sometimes, we need to look at things from a different perspective, with "different eyes," before we can live the gospel for others.

Leader: •Was there ever a time in your ministry when you needed to change your perspective in order to be more effective?

•Are there opportunities within our congregation to alter our perspective so that we can use the gifts of the Spirit more effectively? Perhaps for youth? The separated and divorced? Those grieving the death of a loved one? Those with a relative in prison or trapped by addictions? The addicts themselves?

•What is our perspective toward lay ministers? The parish staff? The clergy? Can they be better served if we look at life through their eyes?

Closing Prayer

All: Almighty God, we sing your praises with joy and thank you for revealing yourself to us as a loving God! Nurturing Lord, we thank you for the mystery of the eucharist which keeps us joined to you. Generous Spirit, we implore your wisdom as we discern the truth and direction in building your kingdom. We make our prayer in a spirit of trust and confidence. Amen.

Prayer at the End of the Meeting

All: Dear God, we believe that where two or more are gathered in your name, you are in our midst. We believe that we have encountered you in our gathering tonight. May this encounter reach deeply into our hearts as we leave this place and touch the lives of others. That we may be signs of the presence of the Spirit, we pray now and always. Amen.

Reprinted with permission from *Weekly Prayer Services for Parish Meetings, Cycle C.* © 1994 *Catholic Herald,* Archdiocese of Milwaukee. Twenty-Third Publications, P.O. Box 180, Mystic, CT 06355. 800-321-0411

Trinity Sunday

Call to Prayer

All: O Lord, our God, how wonderful your name in all the earth!

Leader: When we behold your heavens, the work of your fingers, the moon and the stars which you set in place—Who are we that you should be mindful of us?

All: O Lord, our God, how wonderful your name in all the earth!

Leader: You have made us little less than the angels, and crowned us with glory and honor. You have given us rule over the works of your hands, putting all things under our feet!

All: O Lord, our God, how wonderful your name in all the earth!

Leader: All sheep and oxen, yes, and the beasts of the field, the birds of the air, the fishes of the sea, and whatever swims the paths of the sea.

All: O Lord, our God, how wonderful your name in all the earth!
              (Based on Psalm 8)

Opening Prayer

All: God-Creator, Son-Redeemer, Spirit-Sanctifier, you witness to oneness in three persons. Unite and renew the parish ministers gathered here today. Give us the creative energy to continue your message of truth, the redemptive grace to forgive and reconcile when we are wronged, and the sanctity to always give you reverence. In the name of the Trinity we pray for ever and ever. Amen.

Reading   *John 16:12–15*

Reader 1:   "I still have many things to say to you, but you cannot bear them now. When the Spirit of truth comes, he will guide you into all the truth; for he will not speak on his own, but will speak whatever he hears, and he will declare to you the things that are to come. He will glorify me, because he will take what is mine and declare it to you. All that the Father has is mine. For this reason I said that he will take what is mine and declare it to you." **(Silent reflection)**

Shared Reflection

Reader 2:   The Spirit "will guide you to all truth." The *Decree on the Means of Social Communication* states: "The proper exercise [of communication] demands that the content be true." We all search for truth but many times the truth, or at least how we see the truth, is dependent on perception. The only time we can know and live "truth" is when we communicate and discern what truth really is.

Leader: • Think of an example when perception inaccurately portrayed the truth.

• How can truth be abused or manipulated?

• Can you identify an authentic truth in your life?

Closing Prayer

Leader: God of truth and light, you communicate with us through the testimony of your Son and the prevailing presence of your Spirit. Communicate with us in our thirst to search for your truth in our world. Then give us the courage to express and live it. In the Trinity we pray, God, Jesus, and Spirit, for ever and ever.

All: Amen!

Prayer at the End of the Meeting

All: Dear God, we have encountered you in our gathering tonight. May this encounter reach deeply into our hearts as we leave this place and touch the lives of others. May we be signs of the presence of the God in our world, we pray now and always. Amen.

Reprinted with permission from *Weekly Prayer Services for Parish Meetings, Cycle C.* © 1994 *Catholic Herald*, Archdiocese of Milwaukee. Twenty-Third Publications, P.O. Box 180, Mystic, CT 06355. 800-321-0411

Body and Blood of Christ

Call to Prayer

Leader: We assemble in the name of the Father, and of the Son, and of the Holy Spirit.

All: Amen. Alleluia!

Leader: You servants of the Lord, praise the name of the Lord. (Psalm 113:1)

All: Our hearts rejoice in him; we trust in his holy name. (Psalm 33:21)

Opening Prayer

Leader: Let us pray.

All: Eucharistic Lord, nourish our hearts, minds, and spirits with your presence. Even though we will not commemorate your Last Supper and your sacrificial death this evening, we recall your presence among us when we gather in your name. Make us a eucharistic people, a thankful people, a people willing to give our bodies and our life-blood in service of others. Be with us, eucharistic Lord, now and for ever. Amen.

Reading *Luke 9:11–17*

Reader 1:   When the crowds found out about it, they followed him; and he welcomed them, and spoke to them about the kingdom of God, and healed those who needed to be cured. The day was drawing to a close, and the twelve came to him and said, "Send the crowd away so that they may go into the surrounding villages and countryside, to lodge and get provisions; for we are here in a deserted place." But he said to them, "You give them something to eat." They said, "We have no more than five loaves and two fish—unless we are to go and buy food for all these people." For there were about five thousand men. And he said to his disciples, "Make them sit down in groups of about fifty each." They did so and made them all sit down. And taking the five loaves and the two fish, he looked up to heaven, and blessed and broke them, and gave them to the disciples to set before the crowd. And all ate and were filled. What was left over was gathered up, twelve baskets of broken pieces. **(Silent reflection)**

Shared Reflection

Reader 2:   For this Solemnity of the Body and Blood of Christ, Luke offers a different dimension of eucharist than the expected Last Supper narrative. He tells of super-abundant nourishment. Perhaps it reveals one of the ways we are to live eucharist—by meeting the needs of others through sacrifice, not out of our surplus. We often question how we will find the means to fulfill parish needs with our meager larder. Perhaps the way to increase our parish harvest as well as the number of harvesters is found in the biblical notion of stewardship. Noting that stewardship involves sharing of time and talent as well as treasure, the bishops' pastoral on stewardship notes that stewardship has a eucharistic dimension: "Lived out in the practice of stewardship," it reads, "Christian discipleship can properly be called Eucharistic because it gives thanks to God for the gifts we have received."

Leader: •How do we model good stewardship in our own lives?
•What are some of the ways stewardship in our parish is, or can be, eucharistic?

Closing Prayer

Leader: Heavenly Father, we sing your praise with joy for revealing yourself to us as a loving God! Nurturing Lord, we thank you for the mystery of eucharist which keeps us joined to you. Generous Spirit, we implore your wisdom as we discern truth and direction in building your kingdom.

All: We make this prayer our own as we make the Sign of the Cross and say, In the name of the Father, and of the Son, and of the Holy Spirit. Amen.

Prayer at the End of the Meeting (*Anima Christi*)

All: Soul of Christ, be my sanctification.
Body of Christ, be my salvation.
Blood of Christ, fill all my veins.
Water from Christ's side, wash out my stains.
Passion of Christ, my comfort be.
O Good Jesus, listen to me.
Guard me should the foe assail me.
Call me when my life shall fail me.
Bid me come to you above,
With your saints to sing your love,
World without end. Amen.

Reprinted with permission from *Weekly Prayer Services for Parish Meetings, Cycle C.* © 1994 *Catholic Herald*, Archdiocese of Milwaukee. Twenty-Third Publications, P.O. Box 180, Mystic, CT 06355. 800-321-0411

Tenth Sunday in Ordinary Time

Call to Prayer

Leader: Let us praise and give thanks to the God of our ancestors for all our blessings. **(Pause)**

All: May your love, O Lord, heal and help us, and keep us always on the right path.

Opening Prayer

All: God of all corners of our lives, you are present to us wherever we move and breathe. You find us when we try to hide. You corner us when we stray and lose our connection with you. Be with us now to guide our thoughts so that we may continue your mission of bringing people closer to you. We ask this through Christ our Lord. Amen.

Reading *Galatians 1:11–19*

Reader 1: For I want you to know, brothers and sisters, that the gospel that was proclaimed by me is not of human origin; for I did not receive it from a human source, nor was I taught it, but I received it through a revelation of Jesus Christ. You have heard, no doubt, of my earlier life in Judaism. I was violently persecuting the church of God and was trying to destroy it. I advanced in Judaism beyond many among my people of the same age, for I was far more zealous for the traditions of my ancestors. But when God, who had set me apart before I was born and called me through his grace, was pleased to reveal his Son to me, so that I might proclaim him among the Gentiles, I did not confer with any human being, nor did I go up to Jerusalem to those who were already apostles before me, but I went away at once into Arabia, and afterwards I returned to Damascus. Then after three years I did go up to Jerusalem to visit Cephas and stayed with him fifteen days; but I did not see any other apostle except James the Lord's brother. **(Silent reflection)**

Shared Reflection

Reader 2: With all due respect to religious education teachers, Paul claims he wasn't "taught" the gospel. We all know his story: As he violently destroyed Christians, so he was violently shaken into belief. As we reflect on how we came to faith, we might see that the education we received, while important, did not match the impact of personal experiences and events in bringing us to belief in the good news of Jesus.

Leader: •Was there an event in your life that "knocked you off your feet?" What impact did it have on your faith?

- How can a mishap or tragedy be transformed into a significant faith experience?
- What parish event has so shaken us as a community that our faith has been renewed?

Closing Prayer

All: God of surprises, each time we feel content and protected, you break through our walls to open us again to the wonder and mystery of your life and your love. May we always be brought closer to the one mystery: the new life won for us in the resurrection of your Son, Jesus Christ, our Lord for ever and ever. Amen.

Prayer at the End of the Meeting

Leader: As we leave this meeting to return to our homes, help us to bring the fellowship experienced here to our families and neighbors.

All: Gracious God, keep us in your care, for without you, our lives lose direction and meaning. We ask this through Christ our Lord. Amen.

Reprinted with permission from *Weekly Prayer Services for Parish Meetings, Cycle C.* © 1994 *Catholic Herald*, Archdiocese of Milwaukee. Twenty-Third Publications, P.O. Box 180, Mystic, CT 06355. 800-321-0411

Eleventh Sunday in Ordinary Time

Call to Prayer

Leader: The God of Israel is kind yet firm, compassionate and merciful.

All: Lord God, guide us this day as we bring before you the issues, plans, and programs of the parish.

Opening Prayer

Leader: Loving God, as we gather, direct our thoughts toward you.

All: You sent your Son Jesus to witness to salvation. It is in the little deaths that we endure in our lives every day that we gain a new hope in your power. Your life is within us. We thank you for this gracious gift! Help us as we seek to know your will in all that we do to serve your people. Amen.

Reading *Galatians 2:16, 19–21*

Reader 1: Yet we know that a person is justified not by the works of the law but through faith in Jesus Christ. And we have come to believe in Christ Jesus, so that we might be justified by faith in Christ, and not by doing the works of the law, because no one will be justified by the works of the law. For through the law I died to the law, so that I might live to God. I have been crucified with Christ; and it is no longer I who live, but it is Christ who lives in me. And the life I now live in the flesh I live by faith in the Son of God, who loved me and gave himself for me. I do not nullify the grace of God; for if justification comes through the law, then Christ died for nothing. **(Silent reflection)**

Shared Reflection

Reader 2: In this installment of Paul's letter to the Galatian community (who were Paul's converts), he makes clear that it is faith in Jesus, not the law, that constitutes a "right relationship" with God. It is the law of love that must guide our discipleship.

Leader: •Why do we occasionally get "hung up" on incidentals of the faith?
•What do we have to do to be in "right relationship" with God?
•How powerfully do we as a parish proclaim our faith in Jesus? What sort of letter do you think Saint Paul might write to us?

Closing Prayer

All: God of goodness, may our time together this day reflect the order you have created: Out of nothing comes beauty. May the simple ideas we share have the potential to help our parish community become more faith-filled and dynamic in its service. We ask this through Christ our Lord. Amen.

Prayer at the End of the Meeting

Leader: Together, let us pray as Jesus taught us.

All: Our Father...

(Conclude the meeting by sharing with one another a sign of Christ's peace.)

Reprinted with permission from *Weekly Prayer Services for Parish Meetings, Cycle C.* © 1994 *Catholic Herald,* Archdiocese of Milwaukee. Twenty-Third Publications, P.O. Box 180, Mystic, CT 06355. 800-321-0411

Twelfth Sunday in Ordinary Time

Call to Prayer

Leader: Our God so loved the world that Jesus was sent to be our Savior and win for us the honor of being invited to be priests, prophets, and kings serving one another in the Christian community.

All: May we always live up to this calling in humility and kindness.

Opening Prayer

Leader: Creator God, your world is beautiful to behold, especially at this season.

All: Deepen within us the love and kindness only you can give. May our time together today reflect a small part of your goodness. We ask this through Christ our Lord. Amen.

Reading *Galatians 3:26–29*

Reader 1: For in Christ Jesus you are all children of God through faith. As many of you as were baptized into Christ have clothed yourselves with Christ. There is no longer Jew or Greek, there is no longer slave or free, there is no longer male and female; for all of you are one in Christ Jesus. And if you belong to Christ, then you are Abraham's offspring, heirs according to the promise. **(Silent reflection)**

Shared Reflection

Reader 2: It is good for us to hear this Sunday's second reading from time to time. It reminds us that baptism is so much more than releasing original sin or bringing someone into church membership. Baptism introduces us to the whole world! Through water and other signs, we are connected to the earth in a spiritual way. As the responsibilities of priest, prophet, and king are conferred on us through our baptism into Christ, we receive the call to represent God's love in prayer, teaching, and service.

Leader: •Can you share a time when you felt you truly lived up to one of these responsibilities, even if you were unaware of it at the time?
•How can we help families celebrate baptism and the responsibilities it brings?

Closing Prayer

Leader: Gracious Lord, you told us that to be your followers, we must deny ourselves and take up our cross. How difficult this is at times! We would rather avoid all suffering. Through our prayer, good example, and service to others, we pray that we might prove to be your authentic disciples, in home and workplace, in parish and community.

(Pause for spontaneous prayers.)

Continue to bless us, Lord, as we go about the business of our meeting. Be our shepherd for ever!

All: Amen.

Prayer at the End of the Meeting

Leader: As a reminder of the cross we carry because of our baptismal union with Christ, let us slowly and solemnly make the Sign of the Cross as we say:

All: In the name of the Father, and of the Son, and of the Holy Spirit. Amen.

Reprinted with permission from *Weekly Prayer Services for Parish Meetings, Cycle C.* © 1994 *Catholic Herald,* Archdiocese of Milwaukee. Twenty-Third Publications, P.O. Box 180, Mystic, CT 06355. 800-321-0411

Thirteenth Sunday in Ordinary Time

Call to Prayer

Leader: Heavenly Father, here we are again in "Ordinary Time." Help us to use this time well, Lord. Lead us to the spiritual renewal we need. Revitalize us through each other to complete our summer tasks well as we plan for the coming year. **(Moment of silence)**

Opening Prayer

Leader: Let us pray. Lord, come into our hearts.

All: And make them your own.

Leader: Lord, we praise you for your glory.

All: May our work today bear witness to that praise.

Leader: Lord, we thank you for gifting us to serve you.

All: May we use our gifts to further your kingdom.

Leader: Lord, we ask for guidance.

All: May our deliberations be wise and just.

Reading *Galatians 5:1,13–18*

Reader 1: For freedom Christ has set us free. Stand firm, therefore, and do not submit again to a yoke of slavery. For you were called to freedom, brothers and sisters; only do not use your freedom as an opportunity for self-indulgence, but through love become slaves to one another. For the whole law is summed up in a single commandment, "You shall love your neighbor as yourself." If, however, you bite and devour one another, take care that you are not consumed by one another. Live by the Spirit, I say, and do not gratify the desires of the flesh. For what the flesh desires is opposed to the Spirit, and what the Spirit desires is opposed to the flesh; for these are opposed to each other, to prevent you from doing what you want. But if you are led by the Spirit, you are not subject to the law. **(Silent reflection)**

Shared Reflection

Reader 2: Paul is worried that the Galatians might throw away what they've already gained: freedom in the spirit. Abusing that freedom leads to a new form of slavery—to the flesh. Instead of that he says, "Place yourselves (out of love) at one another's service." Like a wise parent he warns them of the consequences of constant quarreling and highlights the opposition of the flesh and the spirit. Paul says that flesh keeps us from doing the good we'd like to do, making us subject to the law. We must let the Spirit guide us.

Leader: •Should there be a ministry in our parish that fosters reflective listening to people with addictions?

•What are some other problems our parishioners may be facing that are caused by the tug between spirit and flesh?

Closing Prayer

All: Heavenly Father, how awesome is your power over life and death! Sweet Jesus, how eloquent is your example of living what we profess! Holy Spirit, how challenging is your guidance to witness the Word! Triune God, we praise you for revealing yourself to us, for gifting us with faith and the talents to act on that faith, and for providing a vehicle, your church, to spread the Word. Continue to lead us to glorify you, O God, through our work tonight. Enable us to see the vision of your kingdom in glory through the daily dyings and risings that are part of our human experience. In Jesus' name we pray. Amen.

Prayer for the End of the Meeting

Leader: God of healing, open our hearts to identify those people who struggle with the same problems as ourselves.

(Spontaneous petitions)

Leader: We ask your blessing on all in need.

All: Amen. Amen. Lord hear us. Amen.

Reprinted with permission from *Weekly Prayer Services for Parish Meetings, Cycle C.* © 1994 *Catholic Herald,* Archdiocese of Milwaukee. Twenty-Third Publications, P.O. Box 180, Mystic, CT 06355. 800-321-0411

Fourteenth Sunday in Ordinary Time

Call to Prayer

Leader: Rejoice with me, all you who love God.

All: The power of the Lord will be known to the Lord's servants.

Opening Prayer

Leader: We generally do not carry walking sticks or traveling bags when we do our ministry. We carry the cross of Christ. Let us make the Sign of the Cross and pray together.

All: In the name of the Father, and of the Son, and of the Holy Spirit. Amen. "May I never boast of anything but the cross of our Lord Jesus Christ, by which the world has been crucified to me, and I to the world. From now on, let no one make trouble for me; for I carry the marks of Jesus branded on my body. May the grace of our Lord Jesus Christ be with your spirit, brothers and sisters. Amen." (Galatians 6:14, 17–18)

Reading *Luke 10:1–12, 17–20*

Reader 1: After this the Lord appointed seventy others and sent them on ahead of him in pairs to every town and place where he himself intended to go. He said to them, "The harvest is plentiful, but the laborers are few; therefore ask the Lord of the harvest to send out laborers into his harvest. Go on your way. See, I am sending you out like lambs into the midst of wolves. Carry no purse, no bag, no sandals; and greet no one on the road. Whatever house you enter, first say, 'Peace to this house!' And if anyone is there who shares in peace, your peace will rest on that person; but if not, it will return to you. Remain in the same house, eating and drinking whatever they provide, for the laborer deserves to be paid. Do not move about from house to house. Whenever you enter a town and its people welcome you, eat what is set before you; cure the sick who are there, and say to them, 'The kingdom of God has come near to you.' But whenever you enter a town and they do not welcome you, go out into its streets and say, 'Even the dust of your town that clings to our feet, we wipe off in protest against you. Yet know this: the kingdom of God has come near.' I tell you, on that day it will be more tolerable for Sodom than for that town." The seventy returned with joy, saying, "Lord, in your name even the demons submit to us!" He said to them, "I watched Satan fall from heaven like a flash of lightning. See, I have given you authority to tread on snakes and scorpions, and over all the power of the enemy; and nothing will hurt you. Nevertheless, do not rejoice at this, that the spirits submit to you, but rejoice that your names are written in heaven." **(Silent reflection)**

Shared Reflection

Reader 2:   Luke shows Jesus' concern not only for the ministry but for the ministers. He does not send the disciples out alone, but in pairs. The workers are few but he is grateful for their willingness to serve. At the same time, he reminds them that disciples must be single-minded and uncompromising—they are to take no luggage or sandals; they are to trust in the Lord. Like those first disciples, we might wonder how we will find the means to fulfill our ministry and meet our parish's needs with decreasing resources. Perhaps the way to increase our parish's resources is by promoting the biblical notion of stewardship and explaining the link between discipleship and stewardship as a way to build the kingdom of God.

Leader: •What would you identify as the "tools" you need to be a missionary of the gospel in this parish? (Be careful not to list a bunch of "stuff.")
•Share a definition of stewardship that is meaningful for your life.

Closing Prayer

Leader: Confident in God's love and protection, we offer these intentions.

(Spontaneous petitions)

All: God of peace, hear our prayers for ourselves and those in need throughout the world. Through the words we use and the actions we perform may we always be peacemakers in your name. Guide our deliberations and enable us to be mindful of your call to be your representatives in the world. In the name of the great missionary, Jesus Christ, we pray for ever and ever. Amen.

Prayer at the End of the Meeting

Leader: Rejoice with me all those who love God.

All: The power of the Lord will be known to the Lord's servants.

Leader: Let us go forth in peace to continue the work of the Lord.

All: Thanks be to God.

Reprinted with permission from *Weekly Prayer Services for Parish Meetings, Cycle C.* © 1994 *Catholic Herald,* Archdiocese of Milwaukee. Twenty-Third Publications, P.O. Box 180, Mystic, CT 06355. 800-321-0411

Fifteenth Sunday in Ordinary Time

Call to Prayer

Leader: We begin our meeting by opening our hearts to receive the good news of our God.

All: I pray to you, O LORD, for the time of your favor, O God.
In your great kindness answer me with your constant help.
Answer me, O LORD, for bounteous is your kindness;
In your great mercy turn toward me.
(Based on Psalm 69)

Opening Prayer

Leader: Great and wondrous God, our needs are many. The problems in our world are vast yet you satisfy them all with your love. Sometimes we forget that your love is the ultimate solution and needlessly devise our own plans and schemes.

All: Renew this world with your profound love, O Lord. Teach us that all things are possible if we live in your love. In the name of Jesus, your Son, and the Spirit who is present with us tonight, we pray for ever and ever. Amen.

Reading *Deuteronomy 30:10–14*

Reader 1: [The LORD will again take delight in prospering you, just as he delighted in prospering your ancestors,] when you obey the LORD your God by observing his commandments and decrees that are written in this book of the law, because you turn to the LORD your God with all your heart and with all your soul. Surely, this commandment that I am commanding you today is not too hard for you, nor is it too far away. It is not in heaven, that you should say, "Who will go up to heaven for us, and get it for us so that we may hear it and observe it?" Neither is it beyond the sea, that you should say, "Who will cross to the other side of the sea for us, and get it for us so that we may hear it and observe it?" No, the word is very near to you; it is in your mouth and in your heart for you to observe. **(Silent reflection)**

Shared Reflection

Reader 2: We can make life so complicated! Moses remonstrated with the people to keep the Lord's commands and give their hearts over to his service —surely nothing beyond their capabilities. We, too, are to cultivate a relationship with God for God's plan is "already in our hearts." Not complicated, but not easy either.

Leader: • What kind of cultivation of spiritual life is needed to be in a relationship with God: daily prayer, daily Mass, penance, annual retreats, or something else?

• How does one live a spiritual life in today's world?

Closing Prayer

Leader: God is near to us. God already knows our prayers but asks us to humbly find the words and give them to God.

(Spontaneous petitions)

All: Loving God, when we are afflicted and in pain, let your saving help protect us. We will praise your name in song, and we will glorify you with thanksgiving. The Lord is mindful of the poor, and God's own who are in bonds are never spurned. (Based on Psalm 69)

Prayer at the End of the Meeting

All: Lord, you know our hearts. You created in us the human emotions we need to do your will—love for each other, compassion for those hurting, anger at injustice, joy in knowing you. Help us to see that holiness comes from doing ordinary things extraordinarily well. Open us to the needs of others through prayer. We ask this in Jesus' name. Amen.

Reprinted with permission from *Weekly Prayer Services for Parish Meetings, Cycle C.* © 1994 *Catholic Herald*, Archdiocese of Milwaukee. Twenty-Third Publications, P.O. Box 180, Mystic, CT 06355. 800-321-0411

Sixteenth Sunday in Ordinary Time

Call to Prayer

Leader: We gather today to consider our ministry in a spirit of humility aware of our limitations and our need for divine assistance. **(Moment of silence)**

Opening Prayer

All: Gracious God, in the fullness of time you revealed to your people your son, Jesus. Through his life and ministry he showed those in need the mercy, love, and care of God. And, as if that were not enough, he promised to send the Spirit to continue among us the wonders and revelations of your promises. Be with us today and for ever as Creator, Redeemer, and Sanctifier. Amen.

Reading *Colossians 1:24–28*

Reader 1: I am now rejoicing in my suffering for your sake, and in my flesh I am completing what is lacking in Christ's afflictions for the sake of his body, that is, the church. I became its servant according to God's commission that was given to me for you, to make the word of God fully known, the mystery that has been hidden throughout the ages and generations but has now been revealed to his saints. To them God chose to make known how great among the Gentiles are the riches of the glory of this mystery, which is Christ in you, the hope of glory. It is he whom we proclaim, warning everyone and teaching everyone in all wisdom, so that we may present everyone mature in Christ. **(Silent reflection)**

Shared Reflection

Reader 2: Parish members discover that as volunteers or lay ministers their perception of the church and its mission change as they grow in their ministry and their spirituality. It is as if a light grows brighter and brighter inside them. What often begins as little more than a volunteer project leads to a deeper appreciation of church and mission.

Leader: •Can you identify insights you've gained about the church since you became active in your parish?
•How has God been revealed recently to you or to someone you know?

Closing Prayer

All: Loving God, we are nourished with the company of each other because we know you are truly among us, stimulating and encouraging us to know, love, and serve you better. Prepare us to listen to the words and feelings communicated by all those who speak today. Alert us also to those who listen quietly, for they, too, have much to share. Continue your revelation here among us and through the tasks that lie before us. We ask this through Christ our Lord. Amen.

Prayer at the End of the Meeting

All: Lord, you reveal yourself to us in each other. You show us how much you care for us by giving us the wonderful people in our lives. We have so much for which to be grateful. We praise and bless you for your goodness. Be with us as we go about our daily lives. Amen.

Reprinted with permission from *Weekly Prayer Services for Parish Meetings, Cycle C.* © 1994 *Catholic Herald*, Archdiocese of Milwaukee. Twenty-Third Publications, P.O. Box 180, Mystic, CT 06355. 800-321-0411

Seventeenth Sunday in Ordinary Time

Call to Prayer

Leader: Let us quiet ourselves and realize God is present among us. **(Moment of silence)**

Opening Prayer

Leader: Lord, on the day I called for help, you answered me.

All: Lord, on the day I called for help, you answered me.

Leader: I will give thanks to you, O Lord, with all my heart, in the presence of the angels I will sing your praise; I will worship at your holy temple and give thanks to your name.

All: Lord, on the day I called for help, you answered me.

Leader: Because of your kindness and your truth; for you have made great above all things your name and your promise. When I called you answered me; you built up strength within me.

All: Lord, on the day I called for help, you answered me.

Leader: The Lord is exalted, yet the lowly he sees, and the proud the Lord knows from afar. Though I walk amid distress, you preserve me; against the anger of my enemies you raise your hand.

All: Lord, on the day I called for help, you answered me.
(Based on Psalm 138)

Reading *Luke 11:1–13*

Reader 1: He was praying in a certain place, and after he had finished, one of his disciples said to him, "Lord, teach us to pray, as John taught his disciples." He said to them, "When you pray, say: 'Father, hallowed be your name. Your kingdom come. Give us each day our daily bread. And forgive us our sins, for we ourselves forgive everyone indebted to us. And do not bring us to the time of trial.'" And he said to them, "Suppose one of you has a friend, and you go to him at midnight and say to him, 'Friend, lend me three loaves of bread; for a friend of mine has arrived, and I have nothing to set before him.' And he answers from within, 'Do not bother me; the door has already been locked, and my children are with me in bed; I cannot get up and give you anything.' I tell you, even though he will not get up and give him anything because he is his friend, at least because of his persistence he will get up and give him whatever he needs. So I say to you, ask, and it will be given you; search, and you will find; knock, and the door will be opened for you. For everyone who asks receives, and everyone who searches finds, and for everyone who knocks, the door will be opened. Is there anyone among you who, if your child asks for a fish, will give a snake instead of a fish? Or if the child asks for an egg, will give a scorpion? If you then, who are evil, know how to give good gifts to your children, how much more will the heavenly Father give the Holy Spirit to those who ask him!"**(Silent reflection)**

Shared Reflection

Reader 2: Someone once said there is no such thing as private prayer; all prayer is corporate prayer. In this passage, Jesus teaches his disciples how to ask their heavenly Father for all their needs. The Lord's Prayer is truly a prayer for unity. All Christians hope for the day when we will all be able to say it with the sense that we are one in faith and service to one another.

Leader: • How can "daily bread" be understood beyond eucharistic bread?
• In what ways can this prayer be seen as revolutionary?
• What prayer has proven successful for you?

Closing Prayer

Leader: Let us not petition the one God with our many needs but rather with one desire: to know, love, and serve God better.

(Spontaneous petitions)

All: Creative Lord, loosen in us all the knots, twists, and snarls that keep us from each other—the knots that bind us in disagreements, the twists that occur when we do not listen sincerely to one another, and the snarls that keep us from moving closer to you. We call on you, one God, through Jesus Christ, in the Holy Spirit, for ever and ever. Amen.

Prayer at the End of the Meeting

Leader: What better way to conclude than with the prayer Jesus taught us.

All: Our Father...

Reprinted with permission from *Weekly Prayer Services for Parish Meetings, Cycle C.* © 1994 *Catholic Herald,* Archdiocese of Milwaukee. Twenty-Third Publications, P.O. Box 180, Mystic, CT 06355. 800-321-0411

Eighteenth Sunday in Ordinary Time

Call to Prayer

Leader: Let us open our hearts to the Lord's presence in our world by reflecting on the words of the responsorial psalm for Sunday: "If today you hear God's voice, harden not your hearts." **(Moment of silence)**

Opening Prayer

All: Lord God, we live in a secular society. Christian values and prayerfulness often take second place to profit and pleasure. Creator God, show us your presence in all of creation. Jesus Messiah, strengthen us as we try to live out your teachings. Wisdom Spirit, make us mindful of the Trinity dwelling at the core of our being, now and for ever. Amen.

Reading *Colossians 3:1–5, 9–11*

Reader 1: So if you have been raised with Christ, seek the things that are above, where Christ is, seated at the right hand of God. Set your minds on things that are above, not on things that are on earth, for you have died, and your life is hidden with Christ in God. When Christ who is your life is revealed, then you also will be revealed with him in glory. Put to death, therefore, whatever in you is earthly: fornication, impurity, passion, evil desire, and greed (which is idolatry). Do not lie to one another, seeing that you have stripped off the old self with its practices and have clothed yourself with the new self, which is being renewed in knowledge according to the image of its creator. In that renewal there is no longer Greek or Jew, circumcised and uncircumcised, barbarian, Scythian, slave and free; but Christ is all and in all! **(Silent reflection)**

Shared Reflection

Reader 2: The New Testament reading challenges us to look at our goals and values. The first reading for this Sunday contains the famous line, "Vanity of vanities. All is vanity." There is nothing intrinsically wrong with enjoying modern technology—air-conditioned cars, microwave ovens, technological superhighways, TVs with dozens of channels—as long as we don't let them distract us from the faith which must stand at the core of our being.

Leader: •How do I ensure that there are quiet moments each day away from the hustle and bustle where I can be alone with the Lord?
•Can I name one instance where I (or our parish) said or did something to uphold a Christian value in the face of growing secularism and society's decline of morality?
•What personal "vanity" do I wish that I could overcome?

Closing Prayer

Leader: Mindful that we are not perfect, we pray, Lord, have mercy.

All: Lord, have mercy.

Leader: Knowing that we succumb to our personal vanities, we pray, Lord, have mercy.

All: Lord, have mercy.

Leader: Admitting our failings to God and one another, we pray, Lord, have mercy.

All: Lord, have mercy.

Leader: May Almighty God grant us forgiveness and give us the strength to carry out the Lord's work at our meeting today.

All: Amen.

Prayer at the End of the Meeting

Leader: Let us thank the Lord for our many blessings.

All: Thank you, Lord, for being present with us during this meeting. Let us carry your love to our families, our jobs, and our neighborhoods.

Thank you, Lord, for the example and teachings of your Son Jesus. Strengthen us to set our minds on your kingdom which is both here in our midst and in heaven.

Thank you, Lord, for the magnificence of creation. Teach us to use your gifts wisely and to live in your peace now and for ever. Amen.

Reprinted with permission from *Weekly Prayer Services for Parish Meetings, Cycle C.* © 1994 *Catholic Herald,* Archdiocese of Milwaukee. Twenty-Third Publications, P.O. Box 180, Mystic, CT 06355. 800-321-0411

Nineteenth Sunday in Ordinary Time

Call to Prayer

Leader: We approach harvest time in this ordinary season of the liturgical year. We anticipate reaping the rewards of our labors, being concerned about forces like the weather which we can do nothing about, and feeling a certain sense of satisfaction over our hard work. This cycle—sowing, nurturing, reaping—repeats itself year after year, not only in agriculture but in all our life's work. As we reflect on these seasonal gifts, let us praise God. **(Moment of silence)**

Opening Prayer

All: How wise of you, O Creator, to establish the rhythm of our lives! How generous of you to ennoble our work with the belief that all we do in your name is good! How kind of you to give us special moments and times to look forward to that which helps us through the mundane and gives purpose to the ordinary! Bless the work we will accomplish tonight in Jesus' name. Amen.

Reading *Wisdom 18:6–9*

Reader 1: That night was made known beforehand to our ancestors, so that they might rejoice in sure knowledge of the oaths in which they trusted. The deliverance of the righteous and the destruction of their enemies were expected by your people. For by the same means by which you punished our enemies you called us to yourself and glorified us. For in secret the holy children of good people offered sacrifices, and with one accord agreed to the divine law, so that the saints would share alike the same things, both blessings and dangers; and already they were singing the praises of the ancestors. **(Silent reflection)**

Shared Reflection

Reader 2: Foreshadowing the gospel reading in which Jesus stresses the importance of preparedness, this passage from Wisdom refers to preparing for the Exodus event, when the angel of death passed over the homes of the Israelites, sparing their firstborn while slaying the firstborn of the Egyptians. The Israelites knew beforehand the promises God made to deliver those who put their faith in that same merciful God. God's people did not wait blindly for their salvation, but prepared in secret for the moment of deliverance. How much in our lives must we await, sometimes in secret, preparing all the while?

Leader: •How does our parish help parents prepare for the development of their children?

• What do we do to help young people prepare for their adult life choices?

• How do we assist parishioners in preparing their spiritual lives to accept God's promises?

Closing Prayer

All: Glorious God, you give us what we need. You balance our lives with dark clouds and rainbows, even though there are times when we feel there's too much of one and not enough of the other. Help us to see the larger plan, the long range goal, the big picture. Help us to apply the wisdom of the scriptures to our deliberations tonight, secure in the knowledge that all things work for good to those who believe. In Jesus' name we pray. Amen.

Prayer at the End of the Meeting

All: Loving God, may we bring the spirit of Christ to all our efforts, and may we work with our brothers and sisters at our common task, establishing true love and guiding your creation to perfect fulfillment through Christ our Lord. Amen.

Reprinted with permission from *Weekly Prayer Services for Parish Meetings, Cycle C.* © 1994 *Catholic Herald,* Archdiocese of Milwaukee. Twenty-Third Publications, P.O. Box 180, Mystic, CT 06355. 800-321-0411

Twentieth Sunday in Ordinary Time

Call to Prayer

Leader: Let us begin our prayer time with the challenging words of Jesus taken from this Sunday's gospel (Luke 12:49): "I came to bring fire to the earth." **(Moment of silence)**

Opening Prayer

All: Loving and faithful God, inspire each of us to know the urgency of your call to address the many needs that surround us. Give us the courage and fortitude to respond to the tasks before us according to your will. We pray this through our Lord, Jesus Christ, who lives and rules with you and the Holy Spirit, one God, for ever and ever. Amen.

Reading *Hebrews 12:1–4*

Reader 1: Therefore, since we are surrounded by so great a cloud of witnesses, let us also lay aside every weight and the sin that clings so closely, and let us run with perseverance the race that is set before us, looking to Jesus the pioneer and perfecter of our faith, who for the sake of the joy that was set before him endured the cross, disregarding its shame, and has taken his seat at the right hand of the throne of God. Consider him who endured such hostility against himself from sinners, so that you may not grow weary or lose heart. In your struggle against sin you have not yet resisted to the point of shedding your blood. **(Silent reflection)**

Shared Reflection

Reader 2: The urgency expressed in this scripture passage accurately reflects the traumas of the times in which we live. Our Christian faith challenges us to bring healing and peace to the world around us, but there is so much work to be done, so much good for which to struggle. Our faith also calls us to reflect with Jesus who "inspires and perfects our faith" before we act.

Leader: •What urgent needs face our parish community this day?
•What, in your faith, keeps you from growing despondent and abandoning the struggle?

Closing Prayer

All: All-powerful God, there are many concerns in our families, our parish, our city, and the world. Alone we can do nothing. With your guidance and blessing, we can move mountains. Open us to the problems both in our neighborhoods and in the neighborhoods of others. Give us the enlightenment to respond as creatively as we can. By this, you will know we are your people and you are our God. We make this prayer in a spirit of faith. Amen.

Prayer at the End of the Meeting

Leader: We adjourn with the words Jesus gave us.

All: Our Father...

Reprinted with permission from *Weekly Prayer Services for Parish Meetings, Cycle C.* © 1994 *Catholic Herald,* Archdiocese of Milwaukee. Twenty-Third Publications, P.O. Box 180, Mystic, CT 06355. 800-321-0411

Twenty-First Sunday in Ordinary Time

Call to Prayer

Leader: We begin our prayer time with counsel from the book of Hebrews: "Lift your drooping hands and strengthen your weak knees, and make straight paths for your feet." (Hebrews 12:12–13). **(Moment of silence)**

Opening Prayer

Leader: Merciful God, in you we find our purpose and our hope. Through the life of your Son, Jesus, you teach us how to live our lives. Sometimes we fail; other times we forget. When criticisms come our way, give us the moment's pause to reflect and listen instead of reacting immediately. We ask this through Christ our Lord.

All: Amen.

Reading *Luke 13:22–30*

Reader 1: Jesus went through one town and village after another, teaching as he made his way to Jerusalem. Someone asked him, "Lord, will only a few be saved?" He said to them, "Strive to enter through the narrow door; for many, I tell you, will try to enter and will not be able. When once the owner of the house has got up and shut the door, and you begin to stand outside and to knock at the door, saying, 'Lord, open to us,' then in reply he will say to you, 'I do not know where you come from.' Then you will begin to say, 'We ate and drank with you, and you taught in our streets.' But he will say, 'I do not know where you come from; go away from me, all you evildoers!' There will be weeping and gnashing of teeth when you see Abraham and Isaac and Jacob and all the prophets in the kingdom of God, and you yourselves thrown out. Then people will come from east and west, from north and south, and will eat in the kingdom of God. Indeed, some are last who will be first, and some are first who will be last." **(Silent reflection)**

Shared Reflection

Reader 2: The proverb in the last line of this scripture passage teaches the great paradox of the kingdom: Some who are last will be first and some who are first will be last. Which ones are we? Luke records the urgency in Jesus' voice as he narrates the parable of the locked door and those left "stand(ing) outside knocking." Many will be unable to enter, not because they're fated to be kept out but because they seek to enter too late. They feel they deserve admittance because they ate and drank in Jesus' company and heard him preach. But knowledge alone does not save; faith in Jesus saves us.

Leader: • Do we say "Yes" to the challenge of putting our faith into action or do our actions indicate that we have other priorities?
• How is our community better as a result of our efforts?
• How do we teach parishioners of all ages to build their lives on Christ?
• Is furthering the kingdom our number one priority?

Closing Prayer

All: Glorious God, you give us everything we need. You balance our lives with sunshine and clouds, even though there are times when we feel there's too much of one and not enough of the other. Help us to see the larger plan, the long range goal, the big picture so that we do not get stuck in details or short runs which obscure our judgment. Help us to apply the lessons of life and the Word of your Son as we deliberate to-night, secure in the knowledge that all things work for good to those who believe. In Jesus' name we pray. Amen.

Prayer at the End of the Meeting

All: Loving God in heaven, we are the body of your Son when we take a sincere interest in one another. May the words we choose be kind in the hope of improving our parish and our spirit of unity. May we listen with the patience you have given us. We make this prayer in the name of Jesus Christ, our Lord, who lives and rules with you and the Holy Spirit, one God, for ever and ever. Amen.

Leader: Before we return to our homes, let us pray the words Jesus gave us.

All: Our Father...

Reprinted with permission from *Weekly Prayer Services for Parish Meetings, Cycle C.* © 1994 *Catholic Herald*, Archdiocese of Milwaukee. Twenty-Third Publications, P.O. Box 180, Mystic, CT 06355. 800-321-0411

Twenty-Second Sunday in Ordinary Time

Call to Prayer

Leader: We begin our prayer with these wise words from Sunday's first reading which is taken from the Book of Sirach: "Perform your tasks with humility; then you will be loved by those whom God accepts." (Sirach 3:17) **(Moment of silence)**

Opening Prayer

Leader: Wonderful and gracious God, the entire universe marvels at your power and mercy. You created us a little less than the angels. You have given us so much for which to be thankful that one lifetime is insufficient. Continue, this day and in this place, to deepen our love and respect for you. Continue to open our eyes to the wonder and the hope you constantly place before us. There is no problem too great, no mountain too high, no slander too severe to keep us from being your people and responding to your love. We make this prayer through Christ our Lord.

All: Amen.

Reading *Hebrews 12:18–19, 22–24*

Reader 1: You have not come to something that can be touched, a blazing fire, and darkness, and gloom, and a tempest, and the sound of a trumpet, and a voice whose words made the hearers beg that not another word be spoken to them. But you have come to Mount Zion and to the city of the living God, the heavenly Jerusalem, and to innumerable angels in festal gathering, and to the assembly of the firstborn who are enrolled in heaven, and to God the judge of all, and to the spirits of the righteous made perfect, and to Jesus, the mediator of a new covenant, and to the sprinkled blood that speaks a better word than the blood of Abel. **(Silent reflection)**

Shared Reflection

Reader 2: The rich language of this passage from Hebrews reminds us of a wonderful God. In reflecting on this passage we do not ignore the harsh realities of this world, but, in faith, we also see the reality of hope that colors our lives.

Leader: •Can you identify some hope-filled signs that occurred recently in the parish?
•Is there a personal example of hope from your life that you would like to share?

Closing Prayer

Leader: As our meeting begins, together we pray the Lord's Prayer.

All: Our Father...

Prayer at the End of the Meeting

All: Loving and true God, in the daily living of life, may we never lose sight of the hope and positive signs you show us. Open our eyes to see your beauty, our ears to hear the truth, our hearts to feel that here and now we can appreciate you and anticipate the fullness of your love in heaven. We make this prayer in the name of Jesus Christ, your Son, who lives and rules with you and the Holy Spirit, one God, for ever and ever. Amen.

(Conclude by sharing with one another a sign of God's peace and hope.)

Reprinted with permission from *Weekly Prayer Services for Parish Meetings, Cycle C.* © 1994 *Catholic Herald*, Archdiocese of Milwaukee. Twenty-Third Publications, P.O. Box 180, Mystic, CT 06355. 800-321-0411

Twenty-Third Sunday in Ordinary Time

Call to Prayer

Leader: The refrain from Sunday's responsorial psalm reminds us that "In every age, O Lord, you have been our refuge." We pause as we begin our meeting to be reminded of the strength and support we find in a loving God. **(Moment of silence)**

Opening Prayer

All: God of yesterday, today, and tomorrow, because you live forever we are bound to you in all ways. Our lives are short but they have the potential to see your everlasting mark in all passing things. "For a thousand years in your sight are as yesterday" is the way the psalms recognize your authority and power. As we bring ourselves to you we find the tasks before us to be challenging, but possible because of your assistance. "May the gracious care of the Lord our God be ours; prosper the work of our hands for us!" We pray in the person of Jesus who shares all authority with the Creator and the Spirit, one Lord, for ever and ever. Amen.

Reading *Philemon 9–10, 12–17*

Reader 1:   Yet I would rather appeal to you on the basis of love—and I, Paul, do this as an old man, and now also as a prisoner of Christ Jesus. I am appealing to you for my child, Onesimus, whose father I have become during my imprisonment. I am sending him, that is, my own heart, back to you. I wanted to keep him with me, so that he might be of service to me in your place during my imprisonment for the gospel; but I preferred to do nothing without your consent, in order that your good deed might be voluntary and not something forced. Perhaps this is the reason he was separated from you for a while, so that you might have him back forever, no longer as a slave but more than a slave, a beloved brother—especially to me but how much more to you, both in the flesh and in the Lord. So if you consider me your partner, welcome him as you would welcome me. **(Silent reflection)**

Shared Reflection

Reader 2:   One of the common words in our vocabulary that most often has negative and disturbing connotations is the word "authority." For us, it is perhaps particularly disturbing when used in regard to the church. From the authorities in Rome, to the local chancery and the bishop, to our pastor, authority can mean many things to many people. Paul's letter speaks to us today with such warmth and affection about authority that it would melt the fear in even the most threatened of diocesan employees or parish staff members and volunteers. "I am sending him, that is, my own heart, back to you." Paul is sending someone in his place—a representative, someone who knows his ideas well. Paul expects that this representative will be treated as a full-fledged partner.

Leader: •What positive words can enrich and broaden the understanding of authority?

•How does a parent express authority to his or her children in creative ways?

•How can we make this parish a true partnership in faith, inviting and welcoming all in the name of Christ?

Closing Prayer

Leader: God of authority that frees us, help us identify the needs of the people in this community that we may be for them the presence of your Son in their journey through life and toward you.

(Spontaneous petitions)

All: **(After each petition)** Lord of power and might, hear our gentle prayer.

Prayer at the End of the Meeting

All: We believe in the guidance of the Holy Spirit granting authority to the leaders of this parish. We believe, in our hearts, in the eternal and forgiving love of God who enables us to grow closer to each other. We believe in the power shared with us, allowing us creatively to build our community through the gifts and talents given each member of our parish. We pray for the wisdom to humbly know the mind and heart of God, in the name of the Authority, the Witness of obedience, and the Energy of perseverance—Father, Son, and Spirit. Amen.

Reprinted with permission from *Weekly Prayer Services for Parish Meetings, Cycle C.* © 1994 *Catholic Herald*, Archdiocese of Milwaukee. Twenty-Third Publications, P.O. Box 180, Mystic, CT 06355. 800-321-0411

Twenty-Fourth Sunday in Ordinary Time

Call to Prayer

Leader: We reflect today on how we are a "stiff-necked people" in need of forgiveness and reconciliation. **(Moment of silence)**

Opening Prayer

All: Loving and eternal God, create in each of us a clean heart, a heart that gives praise and glory to your wonder and love. May the word "steadfast" take on new meaning for us in our prayer life. May all the words we use today, Lord, be influenced by your wisdom. May our hearts, contrite and true, be a living sacrifice to you. We make this prayer through Christ our Lord. Amen.

Reading *1 Timothy 1:12–17*

Reader 1: I am grateful to Christ Jesus our Lord, who has strengthened me, because he judged me faithful and appointed me to his service, even though I was formerly a blasphemer, a persecutor, and a man of violence. But I received mercy because I had acted ignorantly in unbelief, and the grace of our Lord overflowed for me with the faith and love that are in Christ Jesus. The saying is sure and worthy of full acceptance, that Christ Jesus came into the world to save sinners—of whom I am the foremost. But for that very reason I received mercy, so that in me, as the foremost, Jesus Christ might display the utmost patience, making me an example to those who would come to believe in him for eternal life. To the King of the ages, immortal, invisible, the only God, be honor and glory for ever and ever. Amen. **(Silent reflection)**

Shared Reflection

Reader 2: It can be most upsetting when someone near and dear to us says or does something that truly hurts us. We consider the action inconsiderate, unkind, or cruel. In a state of disbelief, we may ask ourselves over and over, "How could a person have done such a thing? What could this person have been thinking?" Saint Paul's conversion prompted people to ask those same questions about him. The example of Jesus on the cross gives us an indication of how we should handle such situations. His words of forgiveness, "They know not what they are doing," should be our words in such situations. The wisdom of the Lord's Prayer reinforces for us the courage and risk needed in forgiving others as we are forgiven by God. That's the power of healing.

Leader:	•Can anyone share an episode of disbelief over someone's actions?
	•Is there a recent example of reconciliation in your life?
	•How is this parish group involved in forgiveness and reconciliation?

Closing Prayer

Leader:	We give to God the wounds, hurts, and anger that we sometimes carry and cannot resolve ourselves. Let us identify some of the hurts within our parish, city, and world and give them to God.
	(Spontaneous petitions)
Leader:	We make these prayers through Christ our Lord.
All:	Amen.

Prayer at the End of the Meeting

| Leader: | God of forgiveness and healing, the image from this Sunday's gospel of a father welcoming home the wayward son gives each of us the courage to forgive others in your name. Renew in us a heart that is free of all resentment, anger, and bitterness toward the actions of others. Continue to search our hearts for wounds and hurts. May your healing enable us to witness to others the healing we ourselves receive from you. In the name of the Jesus who asks us to forgive seventy times seven times, we pray his special prayer. |
| All: | Our Father... |

Reprinted with permission from *Weekly Prayer Services for Parish Meetings, Cycle C.* © 1994 *Catholic Herald,* Archdiocese of Milwaukee. Twenty-Third Publications, P.O. Box 180, Mystic, CT 06355. 800-321-0411

Twenty-Fifth Sunday in Ordinary Time

Call to Prayer

Leader: As we begin our prayer time, let us reflect on our call to be faithful, wise, just, and responsible stewards of our blessings and resources. **(Moment of silence)**

Opening Prayer

Leader: Loving and ever-living God, your servants gathered here today give you praise. We call on you to challenge us and, in so doing, grow closer to you and to one another. You raise the lowly to new heights because of your love and faithfulness. Allow us, your servants, to be transformed in that way, for only in our concern for the lowly and the poor will you know we are your people. We pray this through Christ our Lord who lives and reigns with you and the Holy Spirit, one God, for ever and ever.

All: Amen.

Reading *Amos 8:4–7*

Reader 1:   Hear this, you that trample on the needy, and bring to ruin the poor of the land, saying, "When will the new moon be over so that we may sell grain; and the sabbath, so that we may offer wheat for sale? We will make the ephah small and the shekel great, and practice deceit with false balances, buying the poor for silver and the needy for a pair of sandals, and selling the sweepings of the wheat." The Lord has sworn by the pride of Jacob: Surely I will never forget any of their deeds. **(Silent reflection)**

Shared Reflection

Reader 2:   Benjamin Franklin is credited with the old axiom, "Honesty is the best policy." We all like to think of ourselves as honest and good people. We are shocked at those who abuse honesty and we feel satisfaction when jail terms are imposed on them. But before we get too smug, we might consider the root of our honesty. While we believe the root of honesty is integrity and self-respect, many people are honest only because they fear the consequences of getting caught! The prophet Amos mixes Ben Franklin's axiom with a deep regard for one's self. Out of that self-regard, one is respectful, decent, and responsible to others; regardless of whether the risks are high or low. This love of self can be grounded only in the deep, abiding love God has for each of us. Another popular saying worth following is, "So be good for goodness sake."

Leader: •How do we communicate honesty and self-respect in our parish, particularly to young people?

•How does this group reflect honesty in its deliberations?

•To whom should the prophet Amos be directing his proclamation today?

Closing Prayer

Leader: Trusting God, deepen within us a respect and regard for ourselves. Help us to develop the honesty that has its roots in your very being. Teach us to respect ourselves that we may respect others. Guide us toward your truth and honesty. We pray this in the name of Jesus, Our Lord and Brother, for ever and ever.

All: Amen.

Prayer at the End of the Meeting

Leader: Together, as Jesus taught us, we pray.

All: Our Father...

(Depart after sharing a sign of God's peace and hope.)

Reprinted with permission from *Weekly Prayer Services for Parish Meetings, Cycle C.* © 1994 *Catholic Herald,* Archdiocese of Milwaukee. Twenty-Third Publications, P.O. Box 180, Mystic, CT 06355. 800-321-0411

Twenty-Sixth Sunday in Ordinary Time

Call to Prayer

Leader: God chose the weak of the world to shame the strong.

All: He chose the lowborn and despised, and reduced to nothing those who were something.

Leader: So that humankind can do no boasting before God.

All: God it is who has given us life in Christ Jesus. He has made him our wisdom and also our justice, our sanctification, and our redemption. (Based on 1 Corinthians 1:30)

Opening Prayer

Leader: Let us pray.

All: Creator God, out of nothing you created us. You bless and sustain us with all good things. Gathered today in your presence, we call on you to assist us in whatever concerns lay before us. As your son Jesus humbly obeyed your will for him and won for us new life, may we open ourselves to hear your call and guidance. We make this prayer in the name of Jesus Christ, your Son and our Brother, for ever and ever. Amen.

Reading *1 Timothy 6:11–16*

Reader 1:   But as for you, man of God, shun all this; pursue righteousness, godliness, faith, love, endurance, gentleness. Fight the good fight of the faith; take hold of the eternal life, to which you were called and for which you made the good confession in the presence of many witnesses. In the presence of God, who gives life to all things, and of Christ Jesus, who in his testimony before Pontius Pilate made the good confession, I charge you to keep the commandment without spot or blame until the manifestation of our Lord Jesus Christ, which he will bring about at the right time—he who is the blessed and only Sovereign, the King of kings and Lord of lords. It is he alone who has immortality and dwells in unapproachable light, whom no one has ever seen or can see; to him be honor and eternal dominion. Amen. **(Silent reflection)**

Shared Reflection

Reader 2:   Whenever scripture speaks of the wealthy we probably think of those who rarely pay taxes, live in ostentatious mansions with too many bathrooms, and whose only concern is whether the gardener will show up on time for work. Yet, we also know that many Catholics enjoy a standard of living that is more than comfortable. The key is not instantly to act defensively and dismiss scriptural admonitions about wealth, but to pause and pray, to see how each of us can respond in our own ways to those less fortunate and poorer than ourselves in material ways.

Leader: • As a parish, how do we respond to the needs of poor people around us?

• Do we delegate the work to a committee or is there parish-wide involvement?

• What is the difference between helping immediate needs and creating social change? Which is more important?

Closing Prayer

Leader: Let us bow our heads in prayer. **(Moment of silence)**

All: Gracious and kind God, make us mindful of our connection with all humankind, those in our neighborhoods as well as those throughout the world. How we respond to the material needs of others is one sign of our response to you. Open our hearts, not to feel guilty, but to know of our goodness and the potential we have to share it with others. We pray this through Christ our Lord. Amen.

Prayer at the End of the Meeting

Leader: Loving and true God, you sent your Son to remind us of our oneness to all creation. Let not a day pass by when we do not lift our thoughts in prayer for troubled nations and peoples throughout the world. In this way may we be grateful for what we have and respond, as best we can, to those in need. Through the Spirit who binds us together, we pray.

All: Amen.

Reprinted with permission from *Weekly Prayer Services for Parish Meetings, Cycle C.* © 1994 *Catholic Herald*, Archdiocese of Milwaukee. Twenty-Third Publications, P.O. Box 180, Mystic, CT 06355. 800-321-0411

Twenty-Seventh Sunday in Ordinary Time

Call to Prayer

Leader: Mindful of the needs of God's people here in our parish and around the world, we now seek the Lord's discernment as we plan for parish life and activities. **(Moment of silence)**

Opening Prayer

All: Loving and gracious God, gathered in this place we can feel like prisoners. There are so many things to do and our lives are filled with demands, commitments, responsibilities, and duties. Yet, we are here and we place our trust in you. May the time we spend together in deliberating matters of the parish awaken in each of us the mystery of service which both helps your people and allows us to give you glory and praise. We make this prayer in the name of Jesus, your Son, through the Holy Spirit, one God, for ever and ever. Amen.

Reading *2 Timothy 1:6–8, 13–14*

Reader 1: For this reason I remind you to rekindle the gift of God that is within you through the laying on of my hands; for God did not give us a spirit of cowardice, but rather a spirit of power and of love and of self-discipline. Do not be ashamed, then, of the testimony about our Lord or of me his prisoner, but join with me in suffering for the gospel, relying on the power of God. Hold to the standard of sound teaching that you have heard from me, in the faith and love that are in Christ Jesus. Guard the good treasure entrusted to you, with the help of the Holy Spirit living in us. **(Silent reflection)**

Shared Reflection

Reader 2: The image of a prisoner describing commitment to God is intriguing. The word conjures up someone who, after breaking the law, is held against his or her will. A prisoner's day is spent molding a gun from a bar of soap or waiting for a friend to deliver the cake with a file inside. Yet, Paul uses this word more than once to speak of service to God. He may mean there is something alluring to God's call; surely it is freely chosen, but at the same time God has "captured" us with irrepressible love.

Leader: •In terms of your service to this parish, how does the word "prisoner" strike you?
•If you feel the allurement of God, why isn't this "parish prison" filled to capacity?

Closing Prayer

Leader: Let us privately call on the Spirit in a moment of silence. **(Pause)**

All: Loving and caring God, we proudly accept being held captive by you and captivated by your goodness and love. Our free will leads us to know more about you through our reading of scripture, and our own private prayer. May the time we spend together here today bring more people of our parish to know of your love and care in their lives. We make this prayer through Christ our Lord. Amen.

Prayer at the End of the Meeting

Leader: As we depart this place to perform those needed tasks and duties at home, let us say the prayer Jesus gave us.

All: Our Father...

Reprinted with permission from *Weekly Prayer Services for Parish Meetings, Cycle C.* © 1994 *Catholic Herald,* Archdiocese of Milwaukee. Twenty-Third Publications, P.O. Box 180, Mystic, CT 06355. 800-321-0411

Twenty-Eighth Sunday in Ordinary Time

Call to Prayer

Leader: Dear God, so often your ways are not our ways. Strengthen our faith to do your will, especially when the tasks before us seem, at first glance, to be useless or foolish.

Opening Prayer

Leader: Let us pray.

All: Lord God, we trust your inspiration in our lives! We profess our willingness to plunge into the Jordan and we believe totally that we will be made clean.

Reading *2 Kings 5:14–17*

Reader 1: So he went down and immersed himself seven times in the Jordan, according to the word of the man of God; his flesh was restored like the flesh of a young boy, and he was clean. Then he returned to the man of God, he and all his company; he came and stood before him and said, "Now I know that there is no God in all the earth except in Israel; please accept a present from your servant." But he said, "As the Lord lives, whom I serve, I will accept nothing!" He urged him to accept, but he refused. Then Naaman said, "If not, please let two mule-loads of earth be given to your servant; for your servant will no longer offer burnt offering or sacrifice to any god except the Lord." **(Silent reflection)**

Shared Reflection

Reader 2: Imagine the joy of being made whole again, free of a terrible disease! Being cured of leprosy also meant being reunited with one's community, from which the afflicted had been cast out. Other afflictions separate people from their families and communities today. This is an area of ministry which may be neglected in parish life today.

Leader: •Who are the outcasts in our community? Do we ignore them out of fear?
•How does the sacrament of reconciliation heal us and restore us to the community?
•Can you share a story of a "miracle" God worked for you recently?

Closing Prayer

All: Dear Lord, our lives are filled with miracles, large and small. Help us to become more aware of them and to thank you again and again for your bountiful presence in our lives.

Prayer at the End of the Meeting

All: Loving Creator, the privilege of serving here tonight is itself a kind of miracle. We thank you for the good people you've sent into our lives, for their wisdom and faith. Keep us always faithful and ever grateful. Amen.

Reprinted with permission from *Weekly Prayer Services for Parish Meetings, Cycle C.* © 1994 *Catholic Herald,* Archdiocese of Milwaukee. Twenty-Third Publications, P.O. Box 180, Mystic, CT 06355. 800-321-0411

Twenty-Ninth Sunday in Ordinary Time

Call to Prayer

Leader: God raised Jesus from the tomb. His resurrection guarantees our own.

All: You can depend on this:
If we have died with him, We shall also live with him.
If we hold out to the end, We shall also reign with him.

Opening Prayer

Leader: Let us pray.

All: Dear Lord, we earnestly desire to live with you for all eternity. Keep us faithful to the end.

Reading *Exodus 17:8–13*

Reader 1: Then Amalek came and fought with Israel at Rephidim. Moses said to Joshua, "Choose some men for us and go out, fight with Amalek. Tomorrow I will stand on the top of the hill with the staff of God in my hand." So Joshua did as Moses told him, and fought with Amalek, while Moses, Aaron, and Hur went up to the top of the hill. Whenever Moses held up his hand, Israel prevailed; and whenever he lowered his hand, Amalek prevailed. But Moses' hands grew weary; so they took a stone and put it under him, and he sat on it. Aaron and Hur held up his hands, one on one side, and the other on the other side; so his hands were steady until the sun set. And Joshua defeated Amalek and his people with the sword. **(Silent reflection)**

Shared Reflection

Reader 2: Life has a way of wearing us down. We can no longer "hold up our arms." We need support to continue. The movement to form small faith-sharing groups has proven valuable in providing such support to striving Christians where occasionally large, impersonal parishes fail. Small groups of parishioners sharing faith and relating it to their daily concerns can be the arms that strengthen and support individual Christians.

Leader: •When did you, literally or figuratively, hold up the arm of someone who was tired and discouraged?
•In your own spiritual struggle what causes you to grow discouraged and lose your motivation to be "steady till sunset"?
•How do we as a parish support and steady one another?

Closing Prayer

All: Abba, Father, we confidently ask you for an increase in faith. We want to tell you that we believe deeply in you, but we also believe that our faith can never be deep enough. Grant us the grace never to doubt our faith in you as Father, Creator, Provider, one with the Son and the Spirit, now and for ever. Amen.

Prayer at the End of the Meeting

Leader: We believe in God, the Father Almighty, creator of heaven and earth.

All: We believe in Jesus Christ, his only Son, our Lord, who died to save us and whose resurrection guarantees our own. We believe in the Holy Spirit and the Holy Catholic Church. We pray that our faith may never fail. Amen.

Reprinted with permission from *Weekly Prayer Services for Parish Meetings, Cycle C.* © 1994 *Catholic Herald,* Archdiocese of Milwaukee. Twenty-Third Publications, P.O. Box 180, Mystic, CT 06355. 800-321-0411

Thirtieth Sunday in Ordinary Time

Call to Prayer

All: Loving God, we direct our cries to you. We know that you hear the prayers of the lowly, the weak, and the oppressed. We will never cease praying until our cries pierce the clouds and reach the heavens where we believe you judge justly and where you affirm what is right.

Opening Prayer

Leader: Let us pray.

All: Almighty God, we live in your presence in a stance of reverence and faith. You read our hearts and so you know that we love you, believe in you deeply, and desire to serve you well all the days of our life.

Reading   *Sirach 35:9–12,14–15*

Reader 1:   Give to the Most High as he has given to you, and as generously as you can afford. For the Lord is the one who repays, and he will repay you sevenfold. Do not offer him a bribe, for he will not accept it. He will not show partiality to the poor; but he will listen to the prayer of one who is wronged. He will not ignore the supplication of the orphan, or the widow when she pours out her complaint. Do not the tears of the widow run down her cheek as she cries out against the one who causes them to fall? **(Silent reflection)**

Shared Reflection

Reader 2:   "If you want peace, work for justice." These words of Pope Paul VI remain a challenge for us. We do not live in a just world, so our efforts to affirm what is right are crucial, especially our advocacy for those who cannot defend their own human rights. We are assured by God that our efforts and prayers to correct wrongs will be fruitful.

Leader: •While God does not always seem to be a God of justice, can you recall an experience you had when God's justice was evident only in hindsight?
•Are there any widows or orphans in your family, your neighborhood? God seems to have a special concern for widows and orphans. How do you imitate him in this respect? How does the parish community reach out to these people?

Closing Prayer

All: Dear Lord, we gather to our hearts tonight all widows and orphans who have been rejected, left hungry, and neglected by those who fail to heed your request to care for these people. Keep us among those who actively support the individuals who are so tenderly defended by you. Amen.

Prayer at the End of the Meeting

All: At some time in our lives, dear Lord, we all feel like orphans. We feel abandoned or rejected by those to whom we looked for support. We forgive anyone who has rejected us and we beg you, dear Lord, to forgive us for the times we have been guilty of rejecting people in our lives. Amen.

Leader: Let us share with one another a sign of acceptance and peace.

Reprinted with permission from *Weekly Prayer Services for Parish Meetings, Cycle C.* © 1994 *Catholic Herald*, Archdiocese of Milwaukee. Twenty-Third Publications, P.O. Box 180, Mystic, CT 06355. 800-321-0411

Thirty-First Sunday in Ordinary Time

Call to Prayer

Leader: We assemble in the name of the Father, and of the Son, and of the Holy Spirit.

All: Amen!

Leader: You servants of the Lord, praise the name of the Lord.

All: Blessed be the name of the Lord, both now and for ever.

Opening Prayer

All: Lord, we have come together as your people. May our lives always be centered upon you, whose "imperishable spirit is in all things." In all our deliberations at this meeting, help us to hear your Word clearly and keep it well. Amen.

Reading *2 Thessalonians 1:11–2:2*

Reader 1: To this end we always pray for you, asking that our God will make you worthy of his call and will fulfill by his power every good resolve and work of faith, so that the name of our Lord Jesus may be glorified in you, and you in him, according to the grace of our God and the Lord Jesus Christ. As to the coming of our Lord Jesus Christ and our being gathered together to him, we beg you, brothers and sisters, not to be quickly shaken in mind or alarmed, either by spirit or by word or by letter, as though from us, to the effect that the day of the Lord is already here. **(Silent reflection)**

Shared Reflection

Reader 2: Paul's basic intention in this reading is to calm the concerns of some early Christians about the implications of the second coming of Jesus, which they perceived to be imminent. His admonition is easily applied to our own turbulent times: Pray always! Our prayer must not only be constant, but it must be of "honest intention" and be seen as a "work of faith." We will then have no need to be afraid of what is to come, but can live in joy.

Leader: • How can we pray always?
• How can we avoid fear of the future which can paralyze us into inaction?

Closing Prayer (Light a candle to represent God's wisdom.)

Leader: Loving God, help us to identify the fears and concerns that consume us and lead us further from you and each other.

(Spontaneous petitions)

All: God of goodness, hear our prayer requesting your wisdom, protection, and strength. Help us to value the important aspects of our lives: the challenges which show our need for you and each other; the joy of our prayer constantly giving you thanks and praise; the hope and trust which we deepen through our commitments. Inspire us by your Word and guide us along the gentle road that leads to you and your kingdom. We pray in the name of Jesus our Lord. Amen.

Prayer at the End of the Meeting

Leader: O great and exalted God! You alone are immortal, you alone dwell in light inaccessible. In your wisdom, you created the entire universe. You separated the light from the darkness, giving the sun charge of the day; the moon and the stars govern the night. At this very hour, you permit us to come before you with our evening songs of praise and glory. In your love for us, direct our prayers as incense in your sight, and accept them as a delightful fragrance.

All: Throughout the present evening and the night which is to come, fill us with your peace. Clothe us in the armor of light. Give us that sleep which you designed to soothe our weakness, a sleep free of all evil. O Master and Giver of all good things, enable us to remember your name throughout the coming night. Then, gladdened by your joy and enlightened by your precepts, let us rise and glorify your goodness. Amen.

Reprinted with permission from *Weekly Prayer Services for Parish Meetings, Cycle C.* © 1994 *Catholic Herald,* Archdiocese of Milwaukee. Twenty-Third Publications, P.O. Box 180, Mystic, CT 06355. 800-321-0411

Thirty-Second Sunday in Ordinary Time

Call to Prayer

Leader: Dear Lord, perhaps no part of your Word is more mysterious to us than the Book of Revelation. Open our minds and hearts tonight as together we meditate on its teachings.

Opening Prayer

All: Beloved Creator, we stand mute and dumb before all the truths you handed down to us in Revelation. We ask for wisdom, for humility, for faith, as we pursue your truths with open hearts and minds. Guide us, lead us, stay with us.

Reading *Revelation 7:2–4, 9–14*

Reader 1: I saw another angel ascending from the rising of the sun, having the seal of the living God, and he called with a loud voice to the four angels who had been given power to damage earth and sea, saying, "Do not damage the earth or the sea or the trees, until we have marked the servants of our God with a seal on their foreheads." And I heard the number of those who were sealed, one hundred forty-four thousand, sealed out of every tribe of the people of Israel. After this I looked, and there was a great multitude that no one could count, from every nation, from all tribes and peoples and languages, standing before the throne and before the Lamb, robed in white, with palm branches in their hands. They cried out in a loud voice, saying, "Salvation belongs to our God who is seated on the throne, and to the Lamb!" And all the angels stood around the throne and around the elders and the four living creatures, and they fell on their faces before the throne and worshiped God, singing, "Amen! Blessing and glory and wisdom and thanksgiving and honor and power and might be to our God forever and ever! Amen." Then one of the elders addressed me, saying, "Who are these, robed in white, and where have they come from?" I said to him, "Sir, you are the one that knows." Then he said to me, "These are they who have come out of the great ordeal; they have washed their robes and made them white in the blood of the Lamb." **(Silent reflection)**

Shared Reflection

Reader 2: Notice the phrase in this passage: "Do not damage." What a command! Perhaps there is an area in parish life where this admonition is needed. Notice, too, the prayer of the elders: "Blessing and glory and wisdom and thanksgiving and honor and power and might be to our God forever and ever!" Our prayer as parish leaders should include praise and thanksgiving as well as petition.

Leader: •What in our lives is helping us gracefully through the challenges of daily life?

•How do we continue to be worthy members of the Communion of Saints?

Closing Prayer

All: Dear God, help us to remember those words of praise and thanksgiving, of wisdom and power. We do not praise you enough. Help us to change this pattern. Amen.

Prayer at the End of the Meeting

All: Dear God, we praise you, we thank you, we celebrate your wisdom and power. We know you to be a God of power, but also a God of mercy and compassion. For all of your attributes, we praise you now and for ever. Amen.

Reprinted with permission from *Weekly Prayer Services for Parish Meetings, Cycle C*. © 1994 *Catholic Herald*, Archdiocese of Milwaukee. Twenty-Third Publications, P.O. Box 180, Mystic, CT 06355. 800-321-0411

Thirty-Third Sunday in Ordinary Time

Call to Prayer

Leader: We gather here tonight in the spirit of love. As witnesses to God's truth, we commit ourselves to work to bring all believers together in the unity of faith and the fellowship of peace. **(Moment of silence)**

Opening Prayer

All: Eternal and true God, since the beginning of time you have graced us with men and women who testify to your boundless love. Sarah, Abraham, Moses, Ruth, Jeremiah, Rebecca, John the Baptizer, and Mary. These people shaped the community that continues today in this room, in this place. The message is the same now as it was then: to know you, God, as ever-present, ever-persistent, everlasting. Protect us, inspire us, and lead us to continue in their paths for you are our God for all ages. We make this prayer in the name of Jesus, the fulfillment of history, and the Holy Spirit, who has brought us here today, one God, for ever and ever. Amen.

Reading *2 Thessalonians 3:7–12*

Reader 1:   For you yourselves know how you ought to imitate us; we were not idle when we were with you, and we did not eat anyone's bread without paying for it; but with toil and labor we worked night and day, so that we might not burden any of you. This was not because we do not have that right, but in order to give you an example to imitate. For even when we were with you, we gave you this command: Anyone unwilling to work should not eat. For we hear that some of you are living in idleness, mere busybodies, not doing any work. Now such persons we command and exhort in the Lord Jesus Christ to do their work quietly and to earn their own living. **(Silent reflection)**

Shared Reflection

Reader 2:   It can be very tempting for us to model our lives after men and women we know little about—celebrities, entertainers, star athletes, political leaders, or captains of industry. These people often seem to exhibit qualities of confidence, inner strength, and a charm that we would like to incorporate into our lives. There is the saying that imitation is the highest form of flattery. Important figures from scripture can offer just as much of a one-sided glimpse of life as can a movie star. We only see and admire what is shown to us. We need to fill in the gaps and see the whole person, as he or she truly is.

Leader: •Whom do you consider an example for you to imitate from the scriptures? from everyday life?

•What quality is embodied in this parish community that you would like to incorporate into your own life?

Closing Prayer

Leader: As our meeting begins, let us blend our voices in the Lord's Prayer.

All: Our Father...

Prayer at the End of the Meeting

All: Loving God, guide and protector of your people, grant us an unfailing respect for your name, and keep us always in your love. Grant this through our Lord Jesus Christ, your Son, who lives and reigns with you and the Holy Spirit, one God, for ever and ever. Amen.

Reprinted with permission from *Weekly Prayer Services for Parish Meetings, Cycle C.* © 1994 *Catholic Herald*, Archdiocese of Milwaukee. Twenty-Third Publications, P.O. Box 180, Mystic, CT 06355. 800-321-0411

Christ the King

Call to Prayer

Leader: "We give thanks to the Father, who has enabled you to share in the inheritance of the saints in the light. He has rescued us from the power of darkness and transferred us into the kingdom of his beloved Son, in whom we have redemption, the forgiveness of sins." (Colossians 1:12–14) **(Moment of silence)**

Opening Prayer

All: Lord Jesus, King of our hearts, during our time together today, we will try to make you a little more present than you were when we began. Open our eyes, soften our hearts, and loosen our tongues that we might see the wonders and marvels of your kingdom and witness to them through our actions. We make this prayer knowing that you live and reign with the Creator and the Holy Spirit, one God, for ever and ever. Amen.

Reading *Luke 23:35–43*

Reader 1: And the people stood by, watching; but the leaders scoffed at him, saying, "He saved others; let him save himself if he is the Messiah of God, his chosen one!" The soldiers also mocked him, coming up and offering him sour wine, and saying, "If you are the King of the Jews, save yourself!" There was also an inscription over him, "This is the King of the Jews." One of the criminals who were hanged there kept deriding him and saying, "Are you not the Messiah? Save yourself and us!" But the other rebuked him, saying, "Do you not fear God, since you are under the same sentence of condemnation? And we indeed have been condemned justly, for we are getting what we deserve for our deeds, but this man has done nothing wrong." Then he said, "Jesus, remember me when you come into your kingdom." He replied, "Truly I tell you, today you will be with me in Paradise." **(Silent reflection)**

Shared Reflection

Reader 2: With the breakup of the Soviet Union, we are quicker than ever to condemn any government that "lords" power over its people. In our own culture we are constantly made aware of the rights of individuals and groups. We uphold the dignity and freedom of each human person anywhere in the world. Yet, this Sunday we commemorate Jesus as king. There are numerous other titles we attribute to Christ—teacher, master, healer, Messiah, Son of God, Son of Man, Savior. We probably identify with those titles more easily than with the title of king. In his letters, however, Saint Paul speaks strongly about finding strength in weakness, riches through poverty, and peace in turmoil. How can we, as Christians, reconcile this point of view with today's triumphal-sounding feast?

Leader:
- How can triumphal titles help and/or hinder the church?
- How does the maxim, "The greatest is the one who serves the rest," apply to this feast?
- Living in a culture with a strong emphasis on individual rights, what does community mean to you?

Closing Prayer

All: Loving God, you raise up men and women to communicate your truth to us all. The ultimate source of truth is found in Jesus, who is our servant, yet our king. Give your church joy in spirit to follow him. Guide those who believe in you into the way of salvation and peace. We ask this through our Lord Jesus Christ, your Son, who lives and reigns with you and the Holy Spirit, one God, for ever and ever. Amen.

Prayer at the End of the Meeting

Leader: As we prepare to leave this communal place where dialogue and trust are valued, let us take this feeling to our places of work and to our homes. We conclude with the Lord's Prayer.

All: Our Father...

Reprinted with permission from *Weekly Prayer Services for Parish Meetings, Cycle C.* © 1994 *Catholic Herald,* Archdiocese of Milwaukee. Twenty-Third Publications, P.O. Box 180, Mystic, CT 06355. 800-321-0411

Of Related Interest...

Psalm Services for Group Prayer

William Cleary

The ancient psalms of David form the basis for half the prayer services in this book. The other half features original psalms by the author.

ISBN: 0-89622-526-7, 96 pp, $12.95 (order B-58)

Psalm Services for Parish Meetings

William Cleary

The author offers prayer services for otherwise ordinary meeting times, using the scriptural book of psalms and poetic psalms that he has written.

ISBN: 0-89622-510-0, 96 pp, $9.95 (order W-35)

Prayer Services for Catechists and Teacher Meetings

Gwen Costello

This is a resource for proclaimers. Included are thirty services complete prayer experiences that also teach valuable faith lessons.

ISBN: 0-89622-696-4, 72 pp, $12.95 (order M-77)

Weekly Prayer Services for Parish Meetings Year A,B

Marliss Rogers, Editor

Helps parish groups open their meetings in a more prayerful, reflective manner. Services are organized around readings for each Sunday. Simple, profound and easy-to-follow services offer meeting participants a sense of mission and purpose.

ISBN: 0-89622-646-8, 118 pp, $12.95 (order M-34)
ISBN: 0-89622-693-x, 120 pp, $12.95 (order M-75)

Centering Prayers

For Personal and Community Prayer

William Cleary

This is a book of contemporary prayer experiences based on a centering technique that can be used for personal prayer or in group settings.

ISBN: 0-89622-608-5, 144 pp, $9.95 (order M-08)

Available at religious bookstores or from:

TWENTY-THIRD PUBLICATIONS
P.O. Box 180 • Mystic, CT 06355

For a complete list of quality books and videos call:
1 - 8 0 0 - 3 2 1 - 0 4 1 1